Bob Buford's first book, *Halftime*, made a great impact on me. I needed that focused perspective! His sincere commitment to significance in life is an inspiration to many including me. I'm excited about the opportunity to take another journey with Bob in *Game Plan.*

Elvis L. Mason
Managing Partner, Mason Best Company

In *Halftime* Bob Buford deeply struck a chord with thousands of middle-agers who yearn for something more. Now with *Game Plan* he shows them how to find it. Inspired by Buford's own remarkable midlife transition, these two books open a whole new world of possibilities for a generation uniquely positioned to give, and by giving to receive.

William T. Solomon
Chairman of the Board, Austin Industries, Inc.

Bob Buford and I have partnered together in challenges of various kinds for over a decade. I have enormous respect for him. And no one shares his enthusiasm for his *Halftime* insights more than I do. Here's to a scintillating and satisfying Second Half.

Bill Hybels
Senior Pastor, Willow Creek Community Church

If you are in the game and running on empty, *Game Plan* will show you how to find new strength and that elusive feeling of fulfillment. It picks up where *Halftime* left off and leads you to a place of accomplishment that satisfies more than just the ego.

Stephen Arterburn
Minirth-Meier New Life Clinics

Though obviously a very committed Christian, Bob Buford's writings are applicable to individuals of any faith. He appropriately challenges all of us to make a difference in *Halftime* and helps us to develop our individual road map in *Game Plan.* His guidance should give readers the opportunity to fulfill their dreams in a much more significant way than in the first half of their life.

Ronald G. Steinhart
Chairman and Chief Executive Officer, Bank One, Texas

Halftime gave thousands the permission to live and love the second half of their life. *Game Plan* tells you how to do it. This is must reading for all of us swimming through midlife. The wise and practical Bob Buford shows us the way.

Bob Rosen
Healthy Companies

Bob Buford once again encourages us to wake up to what really matters in life, and then challenges us to have the fortitude to plan and live accordingly.

Dennis Bakke
President, The AES Corporation

Bob Buford's *Game Plan* is a powerful sequel to his *Halftime*. It combines common sense and practicality with sincerity, spirituality, and a deep understanding of human nature. Buford can offer important ideas with clarity and conviction, because he walks the talk! His life, his ideals, and his accomplishments serve as a practical proof of what can be achieved by people with guiding objectives of improving themselves and the world around them.

Michael J. Kami
President, Corporate Planning, Inc.

Bob Buford's words, book, wisdom, example and significant work through his life reflect his depth of character—and will enrich and bless each reader of his new book. As Bob states, "the real measure of a person's success in life is not his financial accomplishments, but rather moral integrity and inner character." I am thankful that Bob's life and writings encourage all of us who know him, and inspire us to rededicate our personal lives.

Bruce G. Brookshire
Chairman of the Board, Brookshire Grocery Company

This successor to *Halftime,* his book on stock-taking at midlife, gives you the step-by-step instructions for doing what he had earlier simply recommended. If you are trying to decide what comes next for you, this is the book to help you do it.

William Bridges
Author, Transitions *and* JobShift

If you are in your forties or fifties, you may already be thinking of retirement. Bob Buford looks you in the eye and asks "retire from what, to do what?" In an open and engaging way, *Game Plan* tells us how and why everyone in the middle years of their life needs to change their view of success. Bob's own story of moving from mere achievement to magnified significance is inspiring, but more important, it is also a good map for those eager to embrace the future. So if you'd like to do what you really want to do for the next thirty years or so, reading *Game Plan* is a strategic place to start.

Steve Hayner
President, Intervarsity Christian Fellowship

This book succeeds hugely, in describing the predictable moments of midlife passage, plotting the longitude and latitude of a man or woman's forties and fifties. Buford is this era's cartographer to the human soul.

David G. Bradley
Chairman, The Advisory Board Company

Bob Buford lays out in crystal clear terms those ideologies and lifestyle approaches that make the mature years satisfying and meaningful. He gives a clear vision and sense of direction for a meaningful follow-up to the first half.

Norman Brinker
Chairman, Brinker International

In this book, Bob Buford helps us understand how to implement your game plan for the second half, with a goal-line objective of significance.

C. William Pollard
Chairman of the Board, The ServiceMaster Company

Bob Buford has an uncanny ability to understand the issues and emotions of those grappling with the rest of their lives. *Game Plan* takes the next step from defining the opportunity to making a strategy and taking action.

Leith Anderson
Senior Pastor, Wooddale Church

Bob Buford has done a remarkable job of taking stock at life's intersections, then finding fresh ways to leverage his experiences, energies, and resources in service to others. Many find his insights catalysts for growth.

Harold L. Myra
President and Chief Executive Officer, Christianity Today, Inc.

Bob Buford challenges us to enjoy and appreciate the second half of life's journey. It is our chance to exert our greatest influence. *Game Plan* offers great commonsense instructions to map the way. I highly recommend it.

Carl Sewell
Chairman, Sewell Motor Company
Author, Customers for Life

Game Plan guides us in our efforts to convert good intentions into effective and fulfilling action. It's an invaluable tool to produce results.

J. McDonald Williams
Chairman, The Trammell Crow Company

And from the best-selling *Halftime:*

This inspiring book comes out of the mind and heart of a truly remarkable individual and addresses an enormous need in our society—how to find meaning and fulfillment in the second half of our lives. In short, how to move from success to significance!

Stephen R. Covey
Author, The Seven Habits of Highly Effective People

Halftime by Bob Buford is a radically personal, honestly engaging, deeply moving, and spiritually challenging book. It confronts the reader with the crucial choice between success and fruitfulness, death and life, fear and love. It is a true call to conversion by a man for whom conversion has become an ongoing way of life.

Henri Nouwen
L'Arche Daybreak

This book is for successful people who want more fulfillment in their lives and realize it won't come from the next victory, the next sale, the next conquest, or a significant increase in their bottom line. Let Bob Buford be your guide to make sure your best years are ahead of you.

Ken Blanchard
Co-author of The One Minute Manager

When you know a man has touched the peaks of success in what he does, been in the pit of intense grief and suffering in what he has experienced, and made the resolute choice to serve God with all he has and is, you want to read whatever he might write about his life and thoughts. You want to learn the secrets heaven has whispered to him, to know his soul and walk his path. This book will make all of that possible.

Gordon MacDonald
Senior Pastor, Grace Chapel, Lexington, Massachusetts

According to Bob Buford, the first half of life is a quest for success, the second is a quest for significance. Bob should know: he has achieved the first and is showing us the latter. You'll find this book to be unique, inspiring, and practical. Read it and finish strong!

Max Lucado
Author of When God Whispers Your Name

Winning Strategies for the Second Half of Your Life

BOB BUFORD

Author of *Halftime*

ZondervanPublishingHouse

Grand Rapids, Michigan

A Division of HarperCollins*Publishers*

Game Plan

Requests for information should be addressed to:

ZondervanPublishingHouse
Grand Rapids, Michigan 49530

International Trade Paper Edition 0-310-21658-3

Library of Congress Cataloging-in-Publication Data:

Buford, Bob.
Game plan : winning strategies for the second half of your life / Bob Buford.
p. cm.
Includes bibliographical references.
ISBN: 0-310-21205-7 (hardcover)
1. Middle age—Religious life. 2. Success—Psychological aspects. 3. Self realization. 4. Contentment. I. Title.
BV4579.5.B83 1996
248.8'42—dc21 96-51875
CIP

This edition printed on acid-free paper and meets the American National Standards Institute Z39.48 standard.

Published in association with the literary agency of Wolgemuth & Hyatt, 8012 Brooks Chapel Road #248, Brentwood, TN 37027.

Printed in the United States of America

---

97 98 99 00 01 02 03 04 /❖ DH/ 10 9 8 7 6 5 4 3 2 1

To the people of
Buford Television, Inc.,
Leadership Network,
and
The Drucker Foundation,
with whom I have shared both
success and significance.

Other books by Bob Buford

Halftime

CONTENTS

The Longing Within

An author should never conceive himself as bringing into existence beauty or wisdom which did not exist before, but simply and solely as trying to embody in terms of his own arts some reflection of external beauty and wisdom.

C. S. Lewis

No one who writes a book knows how it will be received. But every author soon enough finds out. Shortly after *Halftime* was released, I began hearing from those who had read it. Lots of them. They all said pretty much the same thing: You told my story.

I have heard from CEOs and midlevel managers, sales executives and school teachers. I have heard from pastors and church leaders who have started *Halftime* study groups in their churches, and from entrepreneurs who want to help me branch out into *Halftime* retreats, seminars, and conferences.

I have heard from enough people to realize I may have scratched a huge itch among a widely diverse group of people. Even more diverse than I might have imagined. When my publisher urged me to write specifically for men, he did not have to twist my arm, for I confess I know very little about the reading interests of women. It didn't seem to matter, for I have heard from many women, too.

Most said I had told their husband's story, but a few said what the men had said: You told my story.

If you have not read *Halftime,* I hope I have sufficiently whetted your appetite, not so much because I want to sell another book, but because *Halftime* sort of sets the table for *Game Plan. Halftime* describes what you are probably feeling if you are between the ages of thirty-five and fifty-five and want to move beyond success in your career to significance for your life. But how do you do that? *Game Plan* will show you how to turn that success into significance, practically speaking. It will introduce you to what I call the most undiscovered zone in American life: a runaway third quarter where you will finally play the game of life as you were designed to play it.

Conventional wisdom holds that the first four decades of your life—the first half—are the most exciting and productive years, and that the remaining years represent first a plateau and then a gradual downhill slide into retirement. I have never been enamored with conventional wisdom and, through a series of events I described in *Halftime,* I challenged the notion that when I hit my fifties, I had better start preparing for the golden years. I discovered something so phenomenal, yet so simple: Beginning sometime in your fourth decade and continuing well beyond age sixty-five, the second half of your life can be your best. I'm not talking about staying active or finding a few pleasant hobbies to keep your mind alert. I am absolutely serious when I say the very *best* years of a person's life await him or her in the second half. It is true for me and for many others I know who have refused to think of the second half as a time of declining energy and preparation for retirement. It can be true for you as well.

In your early twenties, you did what was required to get ahead: you put in long hours, took on extra work, were faster and smarter in order to beat the competition. You hit your thirties going strong and began to reap the rewards of your hard work: promotions, better pay, status, and a garageful of toys to play with during your increased leisure time. As you closed in on your fortieth birthday—for most people it can happen as early as the late thirties and as late as the early fifties—you probably felt a combination of battle fatigue and success panic. You began to realize you couldn't or wouldn't live this way forever.

At least that's what happened to me.

The family business I had inherited was growing at around twenty-five percent each year, and though I had started from the ground up and spent most of my waking hours at work, I had reached the point where running the business successfully gave me the feeling of "been there, done that." Added to this was the fact that I had a wonderful, vibrant marriage and a son who turned out to be one of my greatest heroes.

So why was I feeling so unfulfilled?

As I pointed out in *Halftime,* I was in transition from a life focused on success to one measured by significance. My left foot was planted firmly in the world of doing deals and keeping score; my right foot was in unfamiliar territory—a world filled with more questions than answers. I began listening to that still, small voice gently whispering questions in my ear: How much is enough? What is my truest purpose? How would my life look if it really turned out well? What am I going to do with what I had believed all these years?

As I wrote *Halftime,* I confess I wasn't real sure my own experiences would connect with those of others. I, more than anyone, realize I have been blessed and that most people really do have to work for a living. Now, after hearing from so many different kinds of people, I'm absolutely certain the halftime experience is fairly universal. As Peter Drucker pointed out in the foreword to *Halftime,* " . . . for the first time in history, a very large number of people can expect to be 'successes'—something that in the past was practically unknown."

If you are an entrepreneur and are in your forties, you know that within ten years you can retire comfortably. But you also know you will be young, vibrant, talented, and most important, unwilling to winter with the "old folks" in Florida. You want to do something with the rest of your life that will offer meaning and connect with the real you. You have acquired valuable skills that you would like to keep growing, developing. And there is this altruistic notion simmering inside your soul that you would love to give something back so that the world will be just a little bit better because of you.

This scenario holds true for most professionals. Whether it's sales, law, medicine, education, or another profession, you have paid your dues and are at a point where you really can start thinking, "If I really did what I wanted to do, what would I be doing?"

Halftime described my own transition from success to significance; *Game Plan* is the map to help you navigate *your* journey into this remarkable yet untapped season of growth.

My strategy for a winning second half involved handing my business off to a team of trusted colleagues so I could start working with pastors and leaders of large churches on management and strategy issues. You may not have a business to hand off, and you may not be in a position to walk away from your work. But you will still need a strategy to ensure your second half is your best half. In this book, I explore at least eight optional pathways from success to significance. *Game Plan* will help you develop one that is suited to your needs and your own special circumstances. It is a very personal journey.

In *Halftime,* I invited readers to write their own epitaphs. It is a good exercise, one that dramatically helps you focus on what really matters most to you. If you've never done it, try it soon, for a major task of life's second half is a matter of legacy—leaving something valuable behind. Thinking ahead to our ultimate exit and working backwards tends to help us identify our real priorities and potential contributions.

If your life turned out perfectly, what would it look like? What elements would it include? What would you be doing in five years? In ten years? In the space below, describe your idea of destination, of finally arriving at the point where you can say, "I'm finally doing what I've always dreamed of doing."

By the way, I have left room throughout this book for you to jot down notes or answer questions. Or you may want to keep a notebook for these exercises. Either way, I would encourage you to commit your thoughts to paper so that when you finish this book you'll have your own personal game plan to review and implement.

If it is true that every great adventure begins with one small step, you have just begun the most exciting adventure of your life. Take notes. Talk with your spouse and maybe a few very close and trusted friends about your upcoming journey. Pray and listen. Your life will never be the same—and that ought to be the best news you've read today.

Bob Buford
Still Point Farm

Part 1

Leaving the Field

1

Welcome to Halftime

I am forty-six years old; the father of three children (19, 18, and 13); very happily married, and the CEO of a five million dollar subsidiary of a larger company. I am the classic case described in your book, Halftime.

I grew up in a low income Christian family in a rural Tennessee town. As the only member of my family to attend a four-year college, I set high business goals for myself. I have achieved all of them with the exception of accumulating any wealth. The latter goal no longer seems important.

From a letter in response to *Halftime*

As you approach your fourth decade, you begin to think a lot about who you are and where you are going. It is inevitable, and I believe, universal. Some people approach this period in life pathologically and call it a crisis. I regard it more positively and call it halftime—an interval in a person's life where he or she explores ways to transform their success into significance.

You *do* have a choice—you can have a crisis or a halftime.

Midlife Crisis	Halftime
Fears aging	Looks forward to the future
Anxious, worried	Eager, adrenaline rush
Narrowing of interests	Expanding interests/renaissance
Fatigue, depression	Regeneration, anticipation
Impulsive responses	Strategic thinking
Closed, withdrawn	Open, engaging
Rebellion against other people's agenda	Setting your own agenda
Values security	Security is a myth

My hunch is that once the shock of realizing they aren't twenty years old anymore wears off, halftimers can move quickly away from the language of crisis. True, there are still those middle-aged men who continue to try to look and act like teenagers, but by and large, Boomers have finally grown up. In addition to acquiring a variety of skills and achieving a degree of success, they have discovered that at this ripe midpoint of their lives, they still have tremendous energy, creativity, and intellectual capacity. Consider these facts:

- Most people who are fifty will live another thirty years. The actuarial statistics support this assumption. A woman who is fifty, if she doesn't die of cancer or heart disease, will live to see her ninety-second birthday! Men are only slightly behind in this statistic.
- Most of us will likely have a whole second adulthood our grandparents never had. Life expectancy at the turn of the last century was around fifty.

- The additional years we have been given will be marked by good health, vitality, and the capacity to contribute at a very high level.
- Traditional understandings of retirement will no longer be relevant to a growing number of men and women approaching their sixties.

These facts became exceptionally clear to me a few months ago when I went to the barber shop I have used for years. The founder of this shop, Gordon Abbott, had died at age eighty-two, in itself not an unusual occurrence. However, Gordon had worked at the shop until three months prior to his death, when he became ill. This is a pattern that is becoming the norm and, frankly, one that is immensely appealing to me.

I will never forget that pivotal moment in August 1987 when Peter Drucker told me, "You have thirty years left to live, and they will the best thirty years of your life."

Here sat a man in front of me who was almost exactly thirty years my senior and who, in the previous thirty years of his life, had delivered his best and most productive work. In this case, the medium was the message—living proof of immense productivity and influence in the years beyond the fourth decade.

I was forty-eight then, and have now about completed the first ten years of the thirty he promised. So far, everything he said is true. What I find interesting, however, is that more and more people have accepted an almost revolutionary concept of what it means to be old.

I was speaking in Arizona in front of a group of couples who were in halftime and I asked them to think about how old they would be the day they looked in the mirror and considered themselves an old person. The organizers of this conference had given everyone in the audience a "clicker"—an electronic device that instantly recorded their individual answers to any multiple-choice question. Precisely eighty percent of the audience selected "over seventy-five" as when they would consider themselves old. Whether you agree with it, or are making plans for it, if you are in your forties, you will most likely have ahead of you at least thirty more years of potential contribution on the highest level. To help you get your arms around just how much time you have left, think of what it was like to sign your first thirty-year mortgage. That amount of time seemed like an eternity, didn't it?

When our fathers approached the midpoints of their lives, their big questions revolved around retirement: Can I hold on another twenty years? Will I have enough money to retire? With another thirty to forty years of *increased* potential ahead of us, our big question has become, "What am I going to do with the rest of my life?"

Halftime gives you a chance to answer all those important questions you never had time for. It is a season of "in between" where you purposefully anticipate the second half. It's like a second chance, without the guilt and regret that usually comes in needing one. It is not escape, but engagement; not regret, but renaissance. If you were a machine, it would be called retrofitting—making some adjustments in the original piece of equipment so that it can perform new tasks. If you were a piece of software, it would be called upgrading—same basic package, but with revisions and new features that keep it on the cutting edge. My friend Richard Capen, in his book, *Finish Strong*, calls it "repotting." Take a plant out of its old environment, prune it a bit, and place it in a new environment so that it keeps growing and blossoming.

So, how do you know if you are in halftime?

Age is almost a dead giveaway to determining if someone's in halftime. If you're within a couple of years of forty and have been gainfully employed for at least fifteen years, I would almost bet you're beginning to ask yourself, "Can I keep doing this until I'm sixty-five?" and "Do I *really* want to?" I've known people in their mid-fifties who are just beginning to enter halftime, but for the most part, it's an age thing.

But it's more than chronology. In the introduction to this book, I asked you to imagine how your life would look if it were perfect. If you answered that your life is already pretty close to being perfect, or if you thought the exercise I suggested at the end of that introduction was a colossal waste of your time, you're probably a first halfer. Even if we intuitively know things aren't quite right as we blaze through the first half, we don't have the time or energy to fix them. If that's where you are, you probably need a strategy for next week more than you need one for the rest of your life.

But if envisioning your ideal life caught your attention and perhaps raised even more questions, then you are likely to be in halftime. In fact, for me halftime offered more questions than answers. You are probably in halftime if you've pondered any of the following questions:

- Am I missing something in my life right now that's important to me?
- What am I really passionate about?
- Who am I?
- What do I value?
- What do I want to be doing in ten years? In twenty? What is my unfinished task?
- What gifts has God given me that have been perfected over time?
- What gifts has he given me that I am unable to use now?
- What would it take to allow me to quit my job?

- Could I live on a lower income?
- Why am I feeling so bad when I've got it so good?

Another way to look at halftime is through life's events. First half events include formal education (college and/or grad school), marriage, entrance into a profession, beginning a family, etc. Halftime events usually include landmark reunions (mostly your twenty-fifth high school reunion), children leaving the nest, promotions to a senior status, some dreams coming true and others given up, retirement and/or death of parents. These kinds of events interrupt our routine and make us think about our own future.

There is yet another indicator that a person is approaching halftime, and that is something called "plateauing." You're not growing or declining, but in that zone of discontent. The real danger here is inaction. If you notice the symptoms and do nothing, it will lead to "inner kill," the eventual withering of creativity, initiative, and hope. Here are the symptoms of a life stuck on a plateau:

- Avoiding decision-making
- Daydreaming about early retirement
- Talking about what you're going to do, but never following through
- Lying awake at night; sleepwalking by day
- Being irritable most of the time
- Talking to friends about the same things week after week
- Not learning and having no desire to learn
- Having a scattered lifestyle
- Not desiring to risk or try new things
- Unwilling to take charge of your life; allowing circumstances and others to determine your life, decisions, and directions

- Losing eagerness and anticipation for the future
- Worrying excessively

Halftime is a gift of grace extended for the first time in history to our generation. It need not be denied or avoided, but embraced—even if it includes some discomfort and uncertainty. It is an opportunity, not a crisis. You are "on the shore," and there's a bit of work yet to do before you can launch out into the second half of your life. If you take the time to think and plan, the journey ahead will be immeasurably greater than the one you have just completed.

> Youth is not a period of time. It is a state of mind, a result of the will, a quality of the imagination, a victory of courage over timidity, of the taste of adventure over the love of comfort. A man doesn't grow old because he has lived a certain number of years, he grows old when he deserts his ideal. The years may wrinkle his skin, but deserting his ideal wrinkles his soul. Preoccupations, fears, doubts, and despair are the dust before death. You will remain young as long as you are open to what is beautiful, good, and great, receptive to the messages of other men and women, of nature and of God. If one day you should become bitter, pessimistic and gnawed by despair, may God have mercy on your old man's soul.
>
> **Gen. Douglas MacArthur**

2

Reading Your Story

The past is prologue.

From a sign in front of the National Archives, Washington, D.C.

Most of us live the first half our lives as if we had walked into a movie theater twenty minutes after the film started rolling: we are not 100 percent sure what the story is all about, but it seems pretty interesting. By the time we figure out what's going on, it's over.

On the other hand, there are those who seem to have gotten to the movie on time and know exactly where it is going. Peggy Wehmeyer, a reporter for ABC News, alerted me to a book called *Leading Minds,* by Howard Gardner and Emma Laskin. Basically, the book takes a look at the lives of several well-known people such as Margaret Thatcher, Martin Luther King, and the like. What the authors concluded was that each of these leaders had a story within them, and that their lives embody that story for themselves and for others as well. In other words, no one who has achieved significance does so on autopilot.

There is a plot—a story within, if you will—that guides them.

It has been quite a while since I took a college literature class, but I recall being taught that most good stories have a theme—a central idea or message that is communicated through the unfolding of the plot. To help you begin to "read" your own story, try to identify the theme that would emerge in stories about the following people:

Ex. Christopher Reeve	*Courage*
Michael Jordan	____________________
Billy Graham	____________________
Mother Theresa	____________________
Colin Powell	____________________
Elizabeth Dole	____________________
O. J. Simpson	____________________
Michael Milken	____________________
Yourself	____________________

Your first half is a story someone else scripts. Its plot revolves around promotions, children, mortgage payments, relocations, cash flow, net worth, and family commitments. It is a good story, but very little about it is uniquely yours. You are reading from a script, but your heart isn't in it, which is why salesmen and other professionals go to motivational seminars—they need to constantly convince themselves that what they are doing is worthwhile. Of course, it *is* worthwhile to translate your skills, training, and personality into a career, to be a responsible parent, to grow your business, and to improve your net worth, but after fifteen to twenty years, this story gets old.

Halftime allows you to get off autopilot—that set of routines that each of us does more from duty than from passion—and look up, around, and inside to find the larger story that is encoded in your being. To discover the story God implanted in your soul when he created you and to see how that fits into his larger story.

There is a tendency to look at that first-half story in negative terms, and that is what leads men into crisis. Such a scenario focuses on guilt and regrets: "I should have spent more time with my family," "I wish I would have turned down that last promotion," "If I had only known then what I know now." The danger in this kind of thinking is that it usually leads to rash or escapist behavior. I think one reason some middle-aged men run off with their twenty-five-year-old secretaries is that they want to rewrite their stories. They cannot get past the mistakes of their first half, so they erase it and try to write a new one. If you read your first-half story as tragedy, midlife becomes only a brief intermission that precedes the eventual decline and fall of your character.

But if you think of your story as an epic—a grand, ambitious journey for a noble cause—you recognize that everything before the intermission was the setup, the necessary series of events to precede the triumphant finale. Everything in the first half—the successes as well as the failures, the good decisions and the lousy ones—prepares you for something better.

Asked in an interview by *The Dallas Morning News* if he had any regrets, General Colin Powell answered, "Oh, what good are regrets? Regrets slow you down. Regrets cause you to fail to pay attention to the future. So I never log, count, or inventory my regrets. I move on."

I frequently find help in the wisdom of the Bible, and in terms of reading life as an epic, the book of Esther is a great example of how God's story intersects with man's for a greater cause. Biblical scholars may cringe, but the first half of Esther's story looks a lot like the American dream: humble beginnings, willingness to learn from others, opportunity with huge risks, and eventually, prestige and success. From an orphan to a queen may not exactly be Horatio Alger, but it's close.

In the fourth chapter of Esther's story we see a convergence of three subplots: Esther's, her nation's, and God's. Up until this point, life for Esther was pretty much on autopilot. She had achieved a position of prestige far greater than she ever could have imagined, and her future looked bright. Then she had her half-time experience—a time when she was forced to look closely at how her story was going to end. Her mentor and benefactor, Mordecai, issued this challenge that ought to resonate in each of us as we read our first-half story: "Who knows but that you have come to royal position for such a time as this?"

While I do not know your first-half story, I can say with reasonable confidence that it has prepared you for something bigger and better in your second half. When I entered halftime, I sensed a need for a change. I was not sure what it would be, but I knew I did not want to continue running a cable television business full-time. I was fortunate to have the benefit of wise counsel from a few trusted friends who helped me read my first-half story and see that everything I had done as an entrepreneur and a businessman was preparation for my second half. Whatever I would do with the rest of my life—however I would achieve significance—it would build on my first-half skills. As it turned out, everything that went into helping me succeed in the first half is a very big part of why I am enjoying my second half so much. I am doing something different, but I am basically the same person, trading on the skills I was given and that I developed along the way.

What you do in your own second-half mission is probably "hidden in plain sight" (to use a phrase from Thomas Merton). You will most likely get at it by mining your story and finding some deep vein of passion that has expanded and contracted over time as circumstances have allowed. For example, Jack Turpin was a championship-level tennis player in college who, after establishing himself in business, founded T Bar M, a sports camp that combines sports instruction with a values-based curriculum for kids. He's now in his mid-sixties, but what he is doing has been in his story for a long, long time.

The extent to which your second half is significant depends on how you read your story up to this point. If you read it as tragedy and focus on the failures, your second half will most likely develop around that same theme. But if you see your story as an epic, you will know that even the most devastating defeat was yet another step toward the higher, noble goal.

To help you see how everything you have done in your first half sets up the rest of your story—how your first half was preparation for a better second half—reflect on the following questions:

- If your story up until now was going to be published in book form, what would its title be?
- If your story was a movie, who would play your role? Why?
- If your story built up to a major achievement you have made, what would that be? Why were you able to reach that achievement?
- If your story was an epic, what noble cause have you been championing? What was the

motivation behind your accomplishments? What remains to be done?

- Describe a scene in your story in which you, the main character, faced a major setback that brought out the best in you. What characteristic or personal quality did this reveal?
- What other setbacks did you face, and what did you learn from them?
- What events in your story foreshadow what lies ahead for you? What parts of your story do you want to leave out in the second half of your life? What parts do you want to include? What remains to be done?
- Who have been the most important people in your story thus far, and what role will they have in the rest of your story?

Half time lets you revise the second half of your story so that it turns out better—so that it aligns itself with the story God implanted on your soul. He has created a grand narrative for you to live out and is determined to prevent you from writing a smaller, less significant part than the one he has already written.

Who knows but what you have arrived at this point in your life for such a time as this?

Now that you have thought about the first half of your story and how it will be a springboard for the second half, list several bullet points for how you would like the rest of your story to read. One technique to help you identify these points would be to ask yourself the question, "What things do I want to accomplish with my life before I am unwilling to contribute anymore?

Below are some examples to jump-start your thinking.

During my second half, I want to:

- negotiate a gradual reduction in my commitments at work so that by age fifty I will be doing "paid" work no more than twenty hours per week;
- build a team of three trusted advisors with whom I can share my half-time dream and my second-half journey;
- send a letter of introduction to ten nonprofit leaders whose work I resonate with, offering to buy lunch and talk about whether there's a role for me in their organization;
- spend one year developing a training program;
- develop partnerships with hardware and software providers;
- raise capital;
- conduct three overseas trips to troubleshoot;
- launch pro bono on-site computer training program to overseas missionaries; and
- take a "vision trip" to another country ... or to the other side of town.

Once you have finished listing all the items you can think of, use this as a "cheat sheet" to tell your second-half story into your dictaphone. Play it back and listen to the plot of your second-half story.

Game Plan Tip

Incorporate reading and reflection into your halftime experience. Your reading list should include at least one good biography of a great leader—more if you can. The stories of the most successful will show you that significance is not accidental. Here are a few biographies that have inspired and instructed me: *The Gospel of Wealth,* by Andrew Carnegie; *The Templeton Plan,* by John Marks Templeton; *Leading Minds,* by Howard Gardner and Emma Laskin (several biographies in one book); and the book of Ecclesiastes from the Old Testament of the Bible. (This is *the* midlife book in the Bible. I read it every year.) I would also recommend *Late Bloomers,* by Brendan Gill, which profiles seventy-five remarkable individuals whose greatest achievements came later in life. What historic person excited your admiration?

3

Your Truest Self

We must be the change we wish to see in the world.

Gandhi

If you could have a job that allowed you to be yourself, what would you be doing? If you could assign yourself the perfect project—the one that matched your skills and desires with the real you, what would that project be?

What I like most about my second half is that I am finally able to be the "me" that's been inside this person, this body I had been living with throughout my first half. That is not to say most people are phonies during the first half. It's just that to achieve success, you often must set aside the real you and bring yourself in line with another agenda. Not a bad agenda, just someone else's.

As I pointed out in *Halftime,* early in life I struggled over two directions I thought I wanted to go with my life: Christian ministry and business. I will never forget that revelation in Miss Mittie Marsh's ninth-grade English class, where I realized that preaching and baptizing was out; making money as a TV executive was in. Ironically, my halftime experience confronted me with almost the same choices. I have absolutely no regrets about choosing business over ministry, nor should you conclude that since you could not be your truest self in the first half, your career choice was a mistake. At the time, going into the family business was as close to my true self as I could probably get. As Cochrane Chase, former chairman of Cochrane Chase Livingstone, wrote in *If I Knew Then What I Know Now*, "In your twenties, you have time. Experiment. Explore.... In your twenties you find out what you like and what you don't like." I am convinced that most of us cannot fully identify our truest selves when we begin our careers. We are just trying to get going.

But sooner or later, we all feel that sense of ennui—the notion that there's more, an ideal part of ourselves that we haven't quite lived up to and into yet. When that set in over my life, I realized my choice between ministry and business was sort of an artificial choice. The real me was somewhere in between. I had a head for business and, quite frankly, loved doing deals and growing my company. But I also had a gnawing realization that there was more to life than hooking more homes up to cable and making money.

SPIRITUAL DNA

I've concluded from looking at hundreds of people and hearing their stories that significance is something bedded deeply within each of us. It's coded into something I call "spiritual DNA." In the second chapter of the New Testament book of Ephesians, right after the wonderful passage that says new life comes by faith and not by works, St. Paul goes on to say that there is a set of good works prepared for us before we are even born. To me, that is the encoding of a life's work or mission that starts to get at the true self. In other words, your soul will always be restless until you somehow bring your real-world life in line with your spiritual DNA. You may have thought your calling was to manage a major account for a big advertising agency, but your truest self is probably something different.

When you left college, your agenda, most likely, was to get a job and put to work the skills you learned in school. At the time, this may have seemed like your own agenda, but in reality it was someone else's; it was not your truest self. In essence, you made a Faustian bargain: you decided to give up what was deeply important to you in order to make a living. If you were lucky, you were able to hook up with an organization where your personal objectives were congruent with the objectives of the organization. But eventually the dissonance between your true self and the self you have to be in order to succeed gets to you.

Halftime compels you to discover who that truest self really is and to find ways to release it. This *could* mean you leave advertising for a care-giving position at a hospice for AIDS sufferers, but it more likely means you design the fund-raising program for a variety of nonprofit agencies who work with those who are poor or ill. I do not believe God wires you for advertising and then directs you to social work. Instead, he creates you to be a uniquely gifted person and then whispers suggestions on how to use those gifts for his kingdom. Part of the gifting process is a period of field testing. The gifts I perfected in the laboratory of business are the ones I am now using as a social entrepreneur. I did not view my time in business as preparation for a mission of a higher order, but I am convinced God did.

As you enter halftime, you probably have at least a general sense of who your truest self really is, but the more accurately you identify it, the easier it will be to plan your second-half adventure. I have found that asking questions is a pretty good way to learn, and from Peter Drucker come two questions that will help you get at your truest self.

First, "What have I achieved?" This is basically doing the archeology of your own story, where you sweep the sand aside to look for the buried treasure. Reflecting on your achievements tells you something about your skills, what you've been drawn to, what you're good at. Try to come up with at least five major achievements, and then think about what each of these accomplishments says about who you are.

Achievement	**Conclusion**
____________________	____________________
____________________	____________________
____________________	____________________
____________________	____________________
____________________	____________________

Second, "What am I passionate about?" What touches your heart? When you started fresh out of college, the excitement and fervor with which you attacked your career was not passion as much as it was adrenaline. But as you matured, there were certain things that aroused a great passion within. Millard Fuller was a lawyer in Georgia who might still be practicing law had he not developed a deep, deep concern for the poor from his friend and mentor, Clarence Jordan. Millard went on to found Habitat for Humanity, and devotes all his energy to providing affordable housing for poor people.

Make a list of any causes, concerns, issues, or beliefs in which you have a strong interest. Be specific. If, for example, you volunteer to campaign for the local Republican Party, what specifically draws you to their political views—

which "platforms" arouse the greatest passion in you? Try to identify at least five things you are passionate about:

Things To Which I Gladly Give My Time and Resources

(Those things where I lose track of time; where the hours seem to fly by while I am doing them)

____

____

____

____

____

Now go back over that list and try to isolate the one that stands above the rest—your "bottom line" passion. Then go back up to your list of achievements and begin thinking how the things you are good at relate to the thing you are most passionate about. Remember, you are looking for the true you—the person with whom you would be most comfortable. This is the person you want to be during your second half, so it is important that you approach this search honestly.

WHAT'S IN THE BOX?

Another way of getting at your truest self is to identify what is of singular importance to you. In *Halftime,* I recounted a pivotal experience in my journey to significance. With the help of a brilliant strategic planner, I was asked to draw a box and put inside of it a symbol of what was most important to me. Through a day of interview and discussion, this strategist concluded that I had two symbols competing to be placed in the box: a cross, representing my personal faith in Jesus Christ, and a dollar sign, representing my skill and satisfaction in earning money. He told me that if I wanted to put together an honest plan for the rest of my life, I would have to select one of the symbols—I would have to choose one or the other. It really didn't matter to him which one I chose, but both would not fit; it had to be one.

I chose the cross which, ironically, let me be my truest self: a deeply committed follower of Jesus Christ who enjoys various aspects of the business and organizational world. Once I settled the question of who I really was at the core, my personal mission statement almost wrote itself: to transform the latent energy in American Christianity into active energy. Refined to its essence, I like to think of my mission as 100X. I am to be a multiplier; to multiply the gifts I have been given one hundred times. I was a multiplier in my first half. Now I am a multiplier in my second half.

It is important to note that once I decided what went in the box, I did not become a different person, nor have I abandoned other pursuits. I still travel, read, and spend time with Linda and our other friends. It's just that choosing my primary loyalty brought great clarity to my life.

There is nothing wrong with pursuing a first half that is out of step with your true self. We have all done it, which probably explains why we have such a healthy national economy. In the second half, however, you need to balance your own economy—to align your true self with your life's work. Reflect on the exercises in this chapter and begin thinking about the various symbols that are competing for a place in your box.

4

The Risks and Rewards of the Unfamiliar

The real test of a man is not when he plays the role that he wants for himself, but when he plays the role destiny has for him.

Vaclav Havel

I have not met Jane Slater, but I would like to. At fifty-six, she voluntarily stepped down as the CEO of a major company in the Dallas/Ft. Worth area to become an emergency medical technician in Bozeman, Montana. She traded an executive's salary and the rush of running a multimillion dollar business for a small house, a limited income, and a chance to do something she's always wanted to do.

What is it that you have always wanted to do? And why haven't you done it yet?

Anytime you change directions, there are risks. When you do it at the midpoint of your life, those risks could seem to be prohibitive. One of the reasons, in fact, why so many people hold on to their first-half lifestyle until they retire is that they are afraid of losing all they have gained. Theirs is not an unnatural fear; it is not paranoia. The risks are real. If you leave your company, you will no longer draw a salary and you will most likely lose important fringe benefits such as medical insurance. After spending fifteen to twenty years building a network of people, they may no longer return your phone calls. Also, your current position gives you a power base from which to operate (it is harder to get appointments if you do not have a title behind your name). Everything you have worked so hard to achieve *could* go right out the window. In addition, your second-half journey will most likely follow an unfamiliar pathway, so you may not even know all the risks that lie ahead.

Twenty-five-year-olds may be undaunted by such adventure, but forty-five-year-olds are usually thinking about security. Yet as Peter Drucker has noted, "Risk and security are not in opposition, but parallel." Any life that has vitality carries an element of adventure. To give up adventure is to give up a great deal of what not only makes life interesting, but what gives it a certain destiny or purpose. The risk of the unfamiliar can be unsettling, but it is often balanced with the security in knowing that you are en route to doing and being what God designed for you.

Let me give you an example from my own life. When I was thirty-six, in what I have come to call my first-quarter time-out, I wrote down six things I wanted to do with my life. In order to do them, I had to make some significant changes, including ultimately turning the management of my business over to others and taking the risk that neither the growth path of the business or the thrill of the chase would be so intense. Then at age forty-eight, I experienced three great losses: Linda and I lost our only son in January; in June I almost perished in an airplane accident that claimed the lives of four others; and in October the stock market crashed on the day I was to sign the largest cable television deal in my life (the deal fell through).

This was not a great time to take a risk, but at the same time, when things like this happen you begin to sense there's a reason for all of it—that there's some mission or purpose you've been left on earth to fulfill, and even if there are some bumps along the way, you will not be deterred. It is at this level of calling that we find the only deep and enduring security, because we are bringing our truest selves in line with God's design for our lives. There is risk, to be sure, but there is also the peace that comes in knowing we are finally doing what we were created to do. In my case, the risk brought rewards—today I am living my dream. I believe that is what the psalmist meant when he said "Trust in the Lord . . . and he will give you the desires of your heart." I really believe God is on my side.

In retrospect, the rewards outweighed the risk. But how could I have known that on the front end? I couldn't, but I was fairly certain even failure would have been better than not to have launched out on a second-half mission. The key to that certainty was a very clear sense of direction. I had already decided "what's in the box," and once that was settled, it was easier to commit to what I wanted to do with the rest of my life. Halftime is more than deciding you're tired of your first-half life; it involves some careful thinking about how you want to change and what you want to do with your second half.

IN YOUR WILDEST DREAMS

Knowing that you have from twenty-five to thirty-five productive years ahead of you, how do you want to spend them? What do you really want to do with the rest of your life? If you accomplished nothing else, what four to eight things do you want to do before you die? As you think about your answers, be specific. If you want to start a non-profit corporation, what would its purpose be? Instead of saying, "I want to have enough money to not have to work," specify how much you think you would need.

1.

2.

3.

4.

5.

6.

7.

8.

One way of helping you calculate the risk versus reward balance sheet is to take an honest look at where you will end up in thirty years if you maintain the status quo. If you decide not to pursue some or all of the things you listed above, where would you be? What will you have accomplished?

Looking Ahead	**Age**	**Major Achievement**
Five Years	____	____________________
Ten Years	____	____________________
Fifteen Years	____	____________________
Twenty Years	____	____________________
Twenty-five Years	____	____________________
Thirty Years	____	____________________

Now look back at both lists you have just made. Ask yourself which would be worse: risking losing further success in exchange for potential significance, or doing the same thing you are doing now until you retire with all the benefits that course would bring? Which way do the scales tip? Which looks more appealing to you? And to what degree can you have it both ways? Be honest.

If you are still concerned about risk, remember that you don't have to jump right into the unfamiliar. In fact, most second halfers test the waters before they dive in. Most will (and should) begin their "significance career" in parallel with their current job. This follows the first law of the jungle: "Have another vine in sight before you release the one you have hold of." Before Jane Slater moved to Montana, she volunteered at a local hospital for two years to learn how to be an emergency technician—and to see if she really liked doing it. By the time she was ready to hand over the reins of her business to someone else, she knew she had found her calling. Her friend of more than thirty years told a newspaper reporter, "This fits Jane like a glove." In her second half, Jane Slater became her true self.

As you continue developing your game plan for the second half, refer back to the list of things you want to do with the rest of your life. Begin asking yourself what has to happen before you can do these things? And more important, when can you start? I have learned that while many—I would say most—people in their fourth decade really *do* want to move from success to significance, far too many never get beyond the "want to." My friend Tom Paterson, a wise old hand who has done planning for companies for forty years and who now makes a career of helping second halfers find their life plans, says that beginning is the critical part. He amazed me by telling one of his clients, “It is not what you finish that counts most. It’s what you start.”

What’s keeping *you* from living up to your own highest aspirations, from converting good intentions to results and performance?

5

If It's So Good . . .

Didn't we say to you in Egypt, "Leave us alone; let us serve the Egyptians?" It would have been better for us to serve the Egyptians than to die in the desert!

Exodus 14:12

For 430 years, the people of Israel lived in captivity in Egypt. It wasn't a perfect existence by a long shot, but it offered the kinds of things that cause many to give up some of their independence: security, safety, predictability, a familiar routine. Every day was the same: get up, get the straw, make the bricks, come home, feed the kids, go to bed. Within days of their escape into the wilderness, the Israelites were grumbling, "at least we had three square meals and a place to sleep back in Egypt!"

Even in these post-Cold War days when market economies are spreading across the face of the globe, most people still live under political regimes that are closer to Egyptian tyranny than American democracy. As Americans, we're not, thank God, enslaved to a dictator but to what may be an equally demanding despot: our own choices. Using the great epic of the Bible as metaphor, the first half is like Egypt. We have given up our freedom in exchange for a set of routines that are productive, earn us a living, and get us through the day. We enjoy a set of relationships and a physical environment that is both comfortable and familiar.

There were three stages to the Israelites' journey: leaving home, wandering through the wilderness, and entering the Promised Land. Leaving home is that recognition you begin feeling toward the end of your third decade that you don't want to make bricks for Pharaoh anymore. Halftime is the wilderness experience—sort of a wandering journey in which you try to get your bearings and align your true self with God's design for your life. If you listen and obey, you are shown the way to the Promised Land, a second half that is immeasurably better than Egypt.

Like the people of ancient Israel, however, sometimes it's just too daunting to leave home. A lot of people never make it into the second half because they have grown too stuck in the regularity of making bricks for Pharaoh.

THREE GREAT TEMPTATIONS

Another reason so many people never get to the second half is more of a spiritual issue. The transition from success to significance sometimes shapes itself as a classic battle of good versus evil. That there is evil in the world may be uncomfortable to think about, but there is little question of its reality. Jesus acknowledged the importance of this counterforce by making "deliver us from evil" the last request in the prayer that became known as his own. The forces of evil would like nothing more than to prevent talented, productive people committed to God from becoming their truest selves in service to their Creator. Through God's grace and by listening to his voice, I have become more available for his use than I was in the first half, so it stands to reason that there are forces that would like to prevent that from happening.

The biblical account of Jesus in the wilderness is helpful here because it occurred at a time when the Son of God was about to embark on a career of significance. He was roughly thirty years old and in the midst of a successful career as a carpenter. He had just had a dramatic halftime experience where he had gone off into the wilderness for forty days to fast, pray, be close to God, and think about the nature of his next assignment. And just as he was about to step out on the bridge, here comes the Tempter with the three great temptations anyone faces: the desire for the physical; the desire to do something impressive and spectacular; and the desire for power—lust, pride, and greed. As I have thought about the showstoppers that prevent people from acting on their inner desire to serve others in the second half, these three temptations still seem to be the three big tests that appeal to our self-centered hungers and prevent us from "losing our lives in order to gain our lives."

The first temptation was to ask Jesus, who had to have been hungry, to turn a stone into a loaf of bread. This was a physical temptation, one that for most of us translates into comfort, security, and pleasure. Any one of these can divert us from our mission and basically suck up a lifetime, whether that means two hours a night in front of the television, endless hours adding to your material wealth, or getting caught up in the trap of sexual pleasure outside of marriage. I mean, how many people do you know who never get beyond success because they gave in to the temptation to do anything they wanted to satisfy their physical needs?

The second temptation was for Jesus to leap off the cliff, asking God to send the angels to "bear him up." To me, that is the temptation to do something spectacular; to break all the rules. You see this a lot in the very wealthy, in superstar athletes and politicians, who at the midpoint of their lives undertake some type of adventure or risky behavior. I have nothing against adventure, but it can be intoxicating and divert you from going on to find the one thing that will give your life meaning and significance.

The third and final temptation was for Jesus to gain dominion over all the kingdoms of the earth by first worshiping his Tempter. I think this may be the most seductive temptation: the desire for power. I have seen too many men and women enter the halftime of their lives determined to break out of the rut they're in, only to turn back because they do not want to give up the power they have achieved. They're afraid they will be a nobody if they leave the network they have worked hard to join. They get their identity from their first-half work and cannot conceive of starting over again.

OBSTACLES TO THE SECOND HALF

In addition to these three universal temptations, there are other barriers along the road to significance. In my experience, most people in midlife feel a halftime itch, but they never get out of the first half because they are reluctant to overcome the following obstacles.

Fear of Change

Weight lifters and other athletes are fond of saying, "No pain, no gain." Whenever you change anything, there is pain and discomfort. For the second half to be better, it has to be different, but some people just can't let go of the same old thing they've been doing. Or, as William Bridges says in his best-selling book, *Transitions,* "You have to let go of an old thing before you pick up a new one." The best way to counter this fear of change is to let the new pull you away from the old. Focus on future benefits rather than past comforts.

Being Stuck on a "Paradigm Plateau"

When you're on "paradigm plateau," your identity is on autopilot—you're in a groove with habits and practices that earned you success and respect and that follow the adage, "If it ain't broke, don't fix it." The problem here is that you overstay the party and become almost a caricature of yourself. Eventually you become like the boxer who keeps fighting beyond his prime.

Another manifestation of this obstacle is that you've accepted the paradigm that the second half of life is a time of inevitable decline, decay, and decreased vitality. A lot of people come to the end of the first half and don't take a sabbatical to recover and rethink before moving on. They are tired, they have been working tired for several years, and all they can think of is not working. There's a sense of entitlement, a sense that the second half is a time of travel and leisure, a time when your memories outweigh your dreams (chapter 4).

The best way to break out of this rut is to take an honest look at where you will be if you stay where you are and compare it to where you could be if you were to realize your wildest dreams.

Assuming the Second Half Will Be Easy

When you discover the second half will be just as challenging and engaging as the first—only in new territory—you get discouraged and return home. Lots of people finally get up enough courage to try something different with their lives, but then return to Egypt when they are threatened by tough times. That was the story of the

Israelites. They weren't long into the wilderness before they asked Moses to take them back to Egypt.

The best preparation for this obstacle is the knowledge that anything good takes time. Just as it took several years of learning and hard work to achieve your spot in the first half, there is a learning curve that needs to be mastered in the second half too. It took me eight *years* just to develop my second-half mission statement, and for it to be an exact fit to what I was doing. It is called "dumb tax," and it is inevitable.

Having No Compelling New Destination

It takes more than a desire to escape the first half in order to have a better second half. That is why the transition period of halftime is so important. You need to think very clearly about where it is you want to go, not what it is you want to leave. You need to picture vividly a destination that draws you forward, and you need to build momentum in order to overcome the bumpy parts of the journey.

We're pioneers at this—our own fathers didn't have the opportunity to think about a second adulthood when they were in their forties. In college, people think endlessly about their first half. As the Swiss psychologist Carl Jung has suggested, there should be a university to prepare us for the second half just as there is a university experience to prepare us for the first half. Peter Drucker is right to say that the task of the future is "the education of already well-educated adults." We should take preparing for the second half of life as seriously as we take preparing for the first.

Being Diverted by Everyone Else's Agenda

Be prepared. The minute you let someone know you are looking for meaning in your second half of life, you will receive at least three invitations to serve on someone's board of directors. If you are not careful, you will spend your freedom too quickly, even before you have any real freedom to spend.

Remember, one of the forces driving you out of the first half was the fact that you never got to set and follow your own agenda. If you are not careful, you will simply trade your present company's agenda for someone else's. That's not a second half, but a repeat of the first half. Stay focused and disciplined so that your second half agenda is really yours.

LIFTOFF

All of these barriers to moving from the first half to the second can become a form of gravity. You are really like a rocket, fueled up and ready to go. When your engines are ignited, they will roar against a huge inertia. At first, it will be a tremendous strain to break free of those forces that have held you back. But with every inch that you lift off from the ground, you will also gather speed. Christopher Columbus, whose adventure involved a tiny wooden ship instead of a rocket, may be helpful here: "Nothing that results from human progress is achieved with unanimous consent. And those who are enlightened before the others are condemned to pursue that light in spite of others."

Whether or not you are successful in making the journey from the first half to the second isn't entirely in your hands. What you do have control over is whether you begin and whether you persist in the face of obstacles. Eventually, you will soar past the tower, through the atmosphere, and into the rarefied air of a stratosphere where you won't have to work nearly as hard to stay on course.

The next section tells you how.

Part 2

Creating the Plan

The future is not some place we are going, but one we create. The paths are not found, but made, and the activity of making them changes both the maker and the destination.

John Schaar

One of the marks of success in a football team is the ability to change their game plan as needed at halftime. In the locker room, the coaches look at what went wrong, what went right, and then adjust their game plan so to put them in the best possible position to play a winning second half.

Most of us start out with a pretty basic game plan: land a good position in a company, learn and grow, be further ahead each year. But toward the end of the first half, you realize you can't play this way for the entire game.

Now that you are in halftime, it's time to change your game plan. The material in the following eight chapters may need to be adjusted to fit your own specific needs. But based on my own experience and watching hundreds of others make the journey from the first half to the second, these eight steps will help you have a winning second half.

6

Disengage

My life is hectic! I'm running all day—meetings, phone calls, paperwork, appointments. I push myself to the limit, fall into bed exhausted, and get up early the next morning to do it all again. My output is tremendous; I'm getting a lot done. But I get this feeling inside sometimes, "So what? What are you doing that really counts?" I have to admit, I don't know.

From an advertisement in *Time* magazine

Many people who read *Halftime* want to jump right into the second half. They resonate with all the downsides of the first half, and the thought of a better second half is immensely appealing, especially given the possibility of at least thirty more active, productive years. Time to start over and get it right.

Jumping from the first half into the second would be like a football team staying on the field instead of heading for the locker room at halftime. You really can't have a better second half if you skip halftime. And halftime is more than a time-out; in football, it's usually almost a third of the total time of both the first and second halves. In life, it could be several years.

The first step in your game plan for the second half is to disengage from as many distractions as possible so that you can rest, read, reflect, and recover. The transition from success to significance takes time and requires some distance between you and your first-half hyperactivity. Most people in the first half practically careen around work, family, and community responsibilities, with little time to plan, let alone reflect on what it all means, where it's all going. Henry Kissinger said, "Once you get to Washington you're running on intellectual capital." Life outside the Beltway is like that for many of us. We're using ourselves up. We're depleting our reserves.

In one of his parables, Jesus teaches us about the value of "good soil" that multiplies and is fruitful. This type of soil is broken open or receptive. The other three soils in this familiar parable are hard-packed and crowded. To me, these other three soils represent someone who is just too busy or preoccupied to entertain any new ideas. Some people's lives are like the rocky soil, where a new idea takes root superficially but has no depth. Any new idea or activity becomes just one of many good things which are never allowed to grow. For others, their lives are like the soil that is choked by thorns, which Jesus describes as the cares and concerns of this world and the deceitfulness of riches.

One of the great American tragedies is that so many good seeds are planted that eventually become stunted and therefore unfruitful. Good soil needs to be left alone for a season. It needs to be open and receptive. Likewise, we need to disengage from the obsessive preoccupation that first-half achievement orientation brings. Most professions reward people who develop a narrower and more focused specialization. That may be good for business, but it's lousy from a human perspective. I find that I need to retreat weekly to become quiet, to listen to the still, small voice within, to be with Linda, so that I can enlarge my vision. In his infinite wisdom, God provided a Sabbath just for this purpose, but for most of us it has become yet another day to get caught up.

Because I do not know your specific situation, I cannot tell you how to disengage other than to suggest you need to find ways to spend time alone. Completely alone. There will be times in the journey ahead when you need to get away with your spouse to share your thinking and get input, and occasionally you will need to bounce some of your thinking off a trusted friend. But at this point, you need some time by yourself with few distractions.

I know this will be hard for any self-respecting Baby Boomer trying to leave the first half, but it's of paramount importance. So I'd like you to list below the three main reasons why you cannot give yourself at least one full day alone and away from your office:

1.

2.

3.

Now, you've been a problem solver most of your working life. You have gotten to where you are today because you have been resourceful in overcoming obstacles. So assume that a client came to you with these three reasons for not being able to attend a special workshop you've planned for him—a workshop that will change his life. How would you convince him that these three reasons can be overcome? Write your arguments below:

1.

2.

3.

Are you convinced yet that you can indeed afford at least a full-day personal retreat to begin planning the best half of your life? Then the best place to start is with that indispensable tool of all first halfers: your daily planner.

PLANNING YOUR HALFTIME RETREAT

Try to find a full day within the next six weeks when you can make an appointment with yourself. If possible, make it a regular working day, but if that's impractical, set aside a weekend day. Use whatever symbol or designation necessary to remind yourself (and your secretary) that you cannot break this appointment for anything. This will be the first of several second-half retreats—day-long getaways for the sole purpose of putting distance between you and the present so that you can think about how you want to spend the rest of your life. Try to spend this day away from your office or home. Ideally, try to get out of town the night before and book a room at a hotel in another city to make sure you won't be interrupted or be tempted to use the time to answer your E-mail or go back up to the office.

How you spend this time depends a lot on your own makeup, but for this initial outing, I would recommend all or some of the following:

Pray and Listen

Prayer really gets the short shrift in the first half. If we pray at all, it is usually on the run or in the midst of a crisis. I suspect it is no mere coincidence that all the twelve-step programs begin with a "higher power." In many ways, the second half is like recovery—you will not make the journey successfully alone, and prayer is God's gift allowing us to communicate with him.

Most of us talk too much when we pray, which is really kind of silly when you think about it. If prayer is a conversation with God, how can we hear what he has to say if we're talking all the time? God often speaks quietly, which suggests we need to be very still in order to hear him. His voice is often a thought, an idea, a possibility that enters our mind and then leaves quickly if we do not capture it.

Read

Most of the reading we are accustomed to is designed to help us get ahead—books and magazines devoted to our careers. Halftime reading should be more reflective, more contemplative. You are trying to find your center, to shift emphasis from what is useful to what is important. The classics, the early church fathers and saints, great epic novels, biographies, and some of the contemporary literature on transitions are good places to start. At the end of this chapter I will list a few books that have been helpful to me and that I think would help anyone in half time.

Reflect

When was the last time you sat still for more than ten minutes and just thought about your life and where it is going? The first half leaves little time to think, and if we have the time, we feel guilty and look for something to do. It may be uncomfortable at first, but find an inviting spot (or take a long walk), put the books and magazines out of your reach, take the phone off the hook, and think for at least one hour on what you have done with what you were given. Think about the quality of your relationships, your family life. Think about your daily work and how you feel about it. Think about where you would like to be in five years. In thirty years. Look up from the rut you are in and see the larger story of your life. Think about your calling, your mission, your legacy.

Record

In *A Thousand Clowns,* by Herb Gardner, we are exhorted to "... own your own days and name them, each one of them, every one of them, or else the years go right by and none of them belong to you." If you've never kept a journal, halftime is the time to start. This isn't a diary where you write down everything you did each day, but a record of your journey into significance. I always keep an inexpensive notebook handy in which I "number the days." If I run across a quote that inspires me or have a thought about the direction my life is going, I write it down. I sometimes write out my prayers, along with what I think God's answers to me are. I believe the physical act of writing these things down solidifies them in your soul and carries you along in your journey. Your journal also becomes a helpful resource as you read over it and reflect on your progress.

Ask Questions

In *Halftime,* I recommended a series of questions that I call the "Halftime Drill" (*Halftime,* 70–73). Here are a few from that list:

- What do I want to be remembered for?
- What about money? How much is enough? If I have more than enough, what purpose do I serve with the excess? If I have less than enough, what am I willing to do to correct that?

- How am I feeling about my career now? Is this what I want to be doing ten years from now?
- Am I living a balanced life? What are the elements in my life that deserve more time?
- What is the primary loyalty in my life?
- Where do I look for inspiration, mentors, and working models for my second half?
- Peter Drucker says that two important needs are self-realization and community. On a scale of one to ten (ten being the highest), how am I doing?

Create Action Items

You know the routine: attend a meeting, listen to reports, discuss the issues, then make a list of action items you are expected to take care of before the next meeting. A list of action items is a good way to make sure all that valuable time in the meeting brings about progress in your company. In the same way, an entire day out of your busy life is valuable time, and you need to make sure it produces benefits. Before you end your personal retreat, write down in your journal or daily planner specific things you need to do to continue your journey. Some of those items may emerge as you proceed through the next chapters, but one item should always be included in this list: the date of the next meeting. Identify a time—probably not an entire day, but maybe several hours—when you will devote some time to working on your game plan.

REGAIN PASSION

One of the striking patterns in Jesus' life was the way he went off by himself, usually before he faced a difficult assignment. I believe he needed that time to regain the passion for his calling, his unique mission. Likewise, we need time alone not only to plan and to think, but to recharge; to be reconnected to our power source.

Another way to disengage is to put yourself in an entirely different zone. I have, for example, been a moderator and participant at the Aspen Institute, in which participants study the most intense and interesting passages from great books. The Trinity Forum uses the same approach, but comes at it from a Christian rather than humanistic perspective. My friend Don Williams went for a two-week study course at Oxford University several years ago and found it quite refreshing. Sometimes we think our best thoughts when we are in a completely different setting. Be creative and adventurous in your efforts to disengage from the cares and concerns of everyday life.

You could probably continue maintaining your first-half lifestyle for several more years and perhaps even climb higher up the corporate ladder. But the reason that is becoming less appealing to you is that you've lost the passion. The "want to" is external; it does not spring forth from the soul.

Remember, your legacy—your "one thing"—was implanted deep within the inner chambers of your very being long ago. As you disengage from the managed chaos that is so much a part of today's business and professional world, you will position yourself to discover this "spiritual DNA" and find ways to restructure your life around it. The key to understanding this true calling is to view your life from a higher platform.

FOLLOW THROUGH

1. List three open dates for your personal halftime retreat:

2. Where do you plan to spend this time (be specific)?

   ____

3. What do you hope to achieve during this one-day time by yourself?

   ____

   ____

   ____

   ____

BOOKS TO TAKE ALONG

Reading (or listening to books on tape) is a great activity for your halftime retreats. Here are a few that have been especially helpful to me:

Seven Habits of Highly Effective People, by Stephen Covey.

In the Name of Jesus, by Henri J. M. Nouwen. The subtitle is "Reflections on Christian Leadership." Henri, who died unexpectedly last year, looks back on his transition from the academic setting that shaped his first half (Harvard, Yale, Notre Dame) to working with the mentally challenged at the L'Arche Communities in Toronto.

Transitions: Making Sense of Life's Changes, by William Bridges. This is the definitive book on transitions. I have given away countless copies and everyone who reads it tells me, "it's like Bridges is reading my mail."

The Age of Unreason and *The Age of Paradox,* by Charles Handy. Sigmoid curves, portfolio work, the doughnut principle—lots of great ideas.

The Paradox of Success, by John R. O'Neil. Why success doesn't fully satisfy and leaves us wishing for more.

Time and the Art of Living, by Robert Grudin. Drawing on philosophy, science, literature, history, personal experience, and his own wide-ranging imagination, Grudin provides a symphony of penetrating insights and observations about time from a variety of angles.

The Choice Is Always Ours, edited by Dorothy Berkley Phillips, Elizabeth Boyden Howes, and Lucille M. Nixon. First published fifty years ago, this beautiful, wise, and searching book—an exemplary guide to spiritual development from a more humanistic perspective—features several hundred carefully chosen selections from such writers as William Blake, Carl Jung, Paul Tillich, Henry Miller, T. S. Eliot, Nikos Kazantzakis, D. H. Lawrence, Rollo May, and others.

7

Self-Assessment

What I lack is to be clear in my mind what I am to do, not what I am to know .... The thing is to understand myself, to see what God really wished me to do ... to find the idea for which I can live and die.

Søren Kierkegaard

I have a feeling that a lot more people would make the leap to "committed Christian," except for one great fear: "If I let God have complete authority over my life, he'll make me start wearing polyester, get a bad haircut, and ring a bell during holidays." In other words, he won't let me be who I really am.

Why would God do that? It just doesn't make sense. For the first half of your life he equipped you with unique gifts and skills and gave you abilities that no one else can duplicate. And then all of the sudden he asks you to do something you've never done before?

I have found that many people are really afraid of Christianity because they think it is all about uniformity and conformity whereas it doesn't take much observation to see that the plan of creation is not one of conformity but of endless diversity. As Gerard Manly Hopkins says in the first line of his poem, *Pied Beauty*, "Glory be to God for dappled things ..."

God designed each of us in two ways, as individuals and as part of a larger body (Rom. 12; 1 Cor. 12). This suggests that each person entering the second half has two tasks: first, to discover who they are as individuals; second, to find a vehicle (a team, an organization) that allows their individuality to flourish as it is strengthened by the unique gifts of others.

God has been preparing you all along for your second-half assignment, and the next step in your second-half game plan is to get a clear picture of what that mission might be. In this chapter, I will borrow heavily from a group of friends who have developed strategies for teaching halftime ideas in seminars, retreats, and workshops. The goal of this chapter is to help you identify those things you are already good at, that you enjoy doing, and that will play a key role in your second half.

The good news is that in your second half, you really get to be *you*!

GO NORTH(WEST), YOUNG MAN!

A common mistake people make when they are in transition between the first and second halves of their lives is to overlook what they are doing and what got them there. Even if you are burned out in your current job, at one point it seemed uniquely suited to your talents, interests, and abilities.

To help you assess your current arsenal of skills, fill out the following:

Current job/position ________________________________

Key responsibilities ______________________________

____

____

____

____

Abilities required (see list below) __________________

____

____

____

____

Abilities

achieving
acting
adapting
addressing
administering
advising
analyzing
anticipating
arbitrating
arranging
ascertaining
assembling
assessing
attaining
auditing
budgeting
building
calculating
charting
checking
classifying
coaching
collecting
communicating
compiling
completing
composing
computing
conceptualizing
conducting
conserving
consolidating
constructing
controlling
coordinating
coping
counseling
creating
deciding
defining
delivering
designing
detailing
detecting
determining
developing
devising
diagnosing
digging
directing
discovering
dispensing
displaying
disproving
dissecting
distributing
diverting
dramatizing
drawing
driving
editing
eliminating
empathizing
enforcing
establishing
estimating
evaluating
examining
expanding
experimenting
explaining
expressing
extracting
filing
financing
fixing
following
formulating
founding
gathering

generating
getting
giving
guiding
handling
having responsibility
heading
helping
hypothesizing
identifying
illustrating
imagining
implementing
improving
improvising
increasing
influencing
informing
initiating
innovating
inspecting
inspiring
installing
instituting
instructing
integrating
interpreting
interviewing
intuiting
inventing
inventorying
investigating
judging
keeping
leading
learning
lecturing
lifting
listening
logging
maintaining
making
managing
manipulating
mediating
meeting
memorizing
mentoring
modeling
monitoring
motivating
navigating
negotiating
observing
obtaining
offering
operating
ordering
organizing
originating
overseeing
painting
perceiving
performing
persuading
photographing
piloting
planning
playing
predicting
preparing
prescribing
presenting
printing
problem-solving
processing
producing
programming
projecting
promoting
proof-reading
protecting
providing
publicizing
purchasing
questioning
raising
reading
realizing
reasoning
receiving
recommending
reconciling
recording
recruiting
reducing
referring
rehabilitizing
relating
remembering
rendering
repairing
reporting
representing
researching
resolving
responding
restoring
retrieving
reviewing
risking
scheduling
selecting
selling
sensing
separating
serving
setting
setting-up
sewing
shaping
sharing
showing
singing
sketching
solving
sorting
speaking
studying
summarizing
supervising
supplying
symbolizing
synergizing
synthesizing
systematizing
taking
talking
teaching
team-building
telling
tending
testing and proving
training
transcribing
translating
traveling
treating
troubleshooting
tutoring
typing
umpiring
understanding
understudying
undertaking
unifying
uniting
upgrading
using
utilizing
verbalizing
washing
weighing
winning
working
writing

Now go back to the "key responsibilities" and place each of them in one of the following quadrants. Do the same for "abilities required."

High Ability/High Satisfaction	**Low Ability/High Satisfaction**
• developing new talent • counseling • mentoring	• long-range planning • prescribing • imagining
High Ability/Low Satisfaction	**Low Ability/Low Satisfaction**
• overseeing $100 million budget • analyzing • formulating	• managing junior staff • directing

The object of this exercise is to help you begin to focus on the areas that will give you the highest return for your physical and emotional energy. Ideally, your second half will find you spending most of your time in the northwest quadrant. In the first half, we all are required to do those things we may be good at but that we do not enjoy. You can only do those things for so long before burnout sets in. In *Halftime,* I asked, "What job would you be willing to do even if you weren't paid for it?" Your answer to that question will probably be found in the northwest quadrant.

TAKE A "MOTIVATIONAL EKG"

This next exercise is also designed to help you see what you really love to do. It is based on the premise that from the very beginning of your life, God uniquely "wired" you for a mission. As you grew and developed, you performed tasks that were, in effect, dry runs for this calling.

First, in the "Accomplishments" column list your achievements that were most rewarding during that period. Then, in the "Most Fulfilling" column list your top ten accomplishments from all periods. Going on, in the "My Contribution" column describe specifically what you were doing (one or two verbs) that made each of these accomplishments so enjoyable (see the previous list of abilities). After that, under "Primary Motivation" choose the two or three motivations that clearly stand out from your history. List a few specifics that demonstrate and affirm each one of these motivations. Finally, under "Abilities" briefly summarize your primary motivations by completing the statement: "I have the ability to . . ."

After you have completed this exercise, share it with your spouse, a friend, or mentor. Look for patterns and begin thinking about how this information can guide you into a second-half calling.

Primary Motivation

Abilities (I have the ability to . . .)

To discover the primary motivated direction of your heart, examine your "My Contribution" column for a common motivational thread. You might find a key verb repeated. See if you can match these with one of the heart-

Self-Assesment

Period	Accomplishments	Most Fulfilling	My Contribution
Grade School Years			
As a Teenager			
Through Mid-Twenties			
Through Thirties			
Through Present			

beats listed under "I love to . . ." below. This is only a partial list. You may need to generate other heartbeats that speak to your design.

Remember these are *all* God-given motivations. Every one of them can be used in effective ministry, almost every one of them can be identified in the ministry of one of the twelve Apostles. Don't be hesitant to identify a basic heartbeat that doesn't seem spiritual. They are only sinful when used selfishly.

I love to . . .

Operate/Maintain:	I love to efficiently maintain something that is already organized.
Design/Develop:	I love to make something out of nothing. I enjoy getting something started from scratch.
Pioneer:	I love to test and try out new concepts. I am not afraid to risk failure.
Organize:	I love to bring order out of chaos. I enjoy organizing something that is already started.
Serve/Help:	I love to assist others in their responsibility. I enjoy helping others succeed.
Acquire/Possess:	I love to shop, collect, or obtain things. I enjoy getting the highest quality for the best price.
Excel:	I love to be the best and make my team the best. I enjoy setting and attaining the highest standard.
Influence:	I love to convert people to my way of thinking. I enjoy shaping the attitudes and behavior of others.
Perform:	I love to be on stage and receive the attention of others.

Improve:	I love to make things better. I enjoy taking something others have designed or started and improve it.
Repair:	I love to fix what is broken or fix what is out of date.
Be in Charge:	I love to lead the way, oversee, and supervise. I enjoy determining how things will be done.
Persevere:	I love to see things to completion. I enjoy persisting at something until it is finished.
Follow Rules:	I love to operate by policies and procedures. I enjoy meeting the expectations of others.
Prevail:	I love to fight for what is right and oppose what is wrong. I enjoy overcoming injustice.

Adapted from Finding a Job You Can Love,
by R. Mattson and A. Miller.

DISCOVERING YOUR PERSONALITY

By the time you enter halftime, your personality is pretty well developed. To pursue a second-half calling that cuts against the grain of your personality just won't work. The following exercise, adapted from *Finding a Job You Can Love*, by R. Mattson and A. Miller, will show you what kind of personality traits *you* think you have. After you have checked your spot on each line, give it to your spouse or a close friend to see if they view you differently. Are there certain activities you ought to avoid in the second half because of your personality? Are there activities that seem to be a perfect match for your personality?

MY PERSONALITY

How Do I See Myself?

Extroverted — Introverted
3 ____________2 ____________1_|_1 ____________2____________3
extreme — mild mild — extreme

Thinker — Feeler
3 ____________2 ____________1_|_1 ____________2____________3
extreme — mild mild — extreme

Routine — Variety
3 ____________2 ____________1_|_1 ____________2____________3
extreme — mild mild — extreme

Self-Controlled — Self-Expressive
3 ____________2 ____________1_|_1 ____________2____________3
extreme — mild mild — extreme

Cooperative — Competitive
3 ____________2 ____________1_|_1 ____________2____________3
extreme — mild mild — extreme

TAKING STOCK

This final exercise will reveal areas in your life that you may need to adjust or improve in order to be up for your second-half mission. Most of this you know intuitively, but there's something about seeing the whole picture that leads to positive action. If any of these areas of your life slip below "fair," I recommend you address them as part of your second-half game plan.

Incidentally, the creator of this next exercise, Jim Warner, has his own interesting halftime story. Several years ago he was a burned-out CEO, running his own company, making money, but restless. He came to visit me at

Still Point Farm to seek advice about selling his company and getting into something that would replace his success with significance. Over a period of a few years he has become an excellent resource for helping people make their midlife transition successfully. He has become particularly successful in facilitating retreats for members of the Young President's Organization. The irony of people who seek to move from success to significance is that they get both.

Whole Life Vital Signs Checklist

Complete this checklist by placing a mark along each numbered line representing where you are relative to the two statements give below each line. Write the number value corresponding to your mark in the space to the left of each numbered line. If a particular line does not apply to you (e.g., you are not married or have no siblings) give yourself a "5" for that line. After you've completed each section (e.g., WORK/VOCATION), total the numbers for the section and write the total in the indicated space. Each total number represents your "vital sign" reading for a section of the checklist. Mark your readings on the Whole Life Vital Signs Graph, which identifies vibrant, healthy, fair, poor, and dangerous readings for each vital sign.

WORK/VOCATION:

_____ 1 . . . . .3 . . . . .5 . . . . .7 9

w-1 ▲ I am either unemployed or could be unemployed in the near future. — I am very secure in my current job or vocation. ▲

_____ 1 . . . . .3 . . . . .5 . . . . .7 9

w-2 ▲ I hate my work. — I love my work. ▲

_____ 1 . . . . .3 . . . . .5 . . . . .7 9

w-3 ▲ I am consumed by my job. — I have my job well under control. ▲

_____ 1 . . . . .3 . . . . .5 . . . . .7 9

w-4 ▲ My job uses little of my talents. — My job fits my talents perfectly. ▲

____ 1 . . . . .3 . . . . .5 . . . . .7 9
w-5 ▲ My job is my identity. My job is only one expression of my identity. ▲

____ 1 . . . . .3 . . . . .5 . . . . .7 9
w-6 ▲ I am addicted to the power, prestige, attention, and perks of my job. I am totally detached from the power, prestige, attention, and perks of my job. ▲

____ 1 . . . . .3 . . . . .5 . . . . .7 9
w-7 ▲ I desperately need the income from my job. The money is nice, but only a part of why I work. ▲

____ 1 . . . . .3 . . . . .5 . . . . .7 9
w-8 ▲ If I lost or left my job, I don't know what else I'd do. I would have no problem finding another fulfilling job or vocation. ▲

____ 1 . . . . .3 . . . . .5 . . . . .7 9
w-9 ▲ No one values my work. My work is deeply valued by others. ▲

____ Total Score for WORK/VOCATION.

MONEY:

____ 1 . . . . .3 . . . . .5 . . . . .7 9
s-1 ▲ I am in a serious financial crisis. I have no financial concerns. ▲

____ 1 . . . . .3 . . . . .5 . . . . .7 9
s-2 ▲ The rest of my life depends on my income stream. I run the rest of my life independent of my income. ▲

____ 1 . . . . .3 . . . . .5 . . . . .7 9
s-3 ▲ I live in fear of being blindsided financially. I have no concerns about being blindsided financially. ▲

_____ 1 . . . . .3 . . . . .5 . . . . .7 9
s-4 ▲ I have no financial reserves if a crisis hits. — I have ample financial reserves if a crisis hits. ▲

_____ 1 . . . . .3 . . . . .5 . . . . .7 9
s-5 ▲ No matter how much I make, I'll never be satisfied. — I'm content with my current income and net worth. ▲

_____ 1 . . . . .3 . . . . .5 . . . . .7 9
s-6 ▲ I feel enormous pressure to make more money. — I feel no pressure to make more money. ▲

_____ 1 . . . . .3 . . . . .5 . . . . .7 9
s-7 ▲ I have great uncertainty about my financial future. — My financial future is secure. ▲

_____ Total Score for MONEY.

MARRIAGE:

_____ 1 . . . . .3 . . . . .5 . . . . .7 9
m-1 ▲ My marriage is about to blow up. — My marriage is very solid. ▲

_____ 1 . . . . .3 . . . . .5 . . . . .7 9
m-2 ▲ My sex life is either awful or nonexistent. — My sex life is very fulfilling. ▲

_____ 1 . . . . .3 . . . . .5 . . . . .7 9
m-3 ▲ We have no meaningful communication. — We communicate the deep issues of our hearts. ▲

_____ 1 . . . . .3 . . . . .5 . . . . .7 9
m-4 ▲ We cannot deal productively with conflict. — We face our conflicts openly and always resolve them. ▲

_____ 1 . . . . .3 . . . . .5 . . . . .7 9
m-5 ▲ We are hopelessly co-dependent. — We are wonderfully interdependent. ▲

_____ 1 . . . . .3 . . . . .5 . . . . .7 9
m-6 ▲ I no longer love my spouse. I am in love with my spouse. ▲

_____ 1 . . . . .3 . . . . .5 . . . . .7 9
m-7 ▲ My spouse no longer loves me. My spouse is very much in love with me. ▲

_____ Total Score for MARRIAGE.

CHILDREN AND EXTENDED FAMILY:

_____ 1 . . . . .3 . . . . .5 . . . . .7 9
cef-1 ▲ One or more of my children is in a major crisis. All my children lead healthy, fulfilled lives. ▲

_____ 1 . . . . .3 . . . . .5 . . . . .7 9
cef-2 ▲ My kids either hate me or avoid me. My kids love me and love to be with me. ▲

_____ 1 . . . . .3 . . . . .5 . . . . .7 9
cef-3 ▲ I don't know my children for who they are. I know my children and love them. ▲

_____ 1 . . . . .3 . . . . .5 . . . . .7 9
cef-4 ▲ I am missing (have missed) my kids growing up. I'm there with my kids as they grow up (grew up). ▲

_____ 1 . . . . .3 . . . . .5 . . . . .7 9
cef-5 ▲ I have major unresolved issues with my parents. I get along (got along) with my parents. ▲

_____ 1 . . . . .3 . . . . .5 . . . . .7 9
cef-6 ▲ I have major unresolved issues with my siblings. I have deep, fulfilling relationships with my siblings. ▲

_____ Total Score for CHILDREN AND EXTENDED FAMILY.

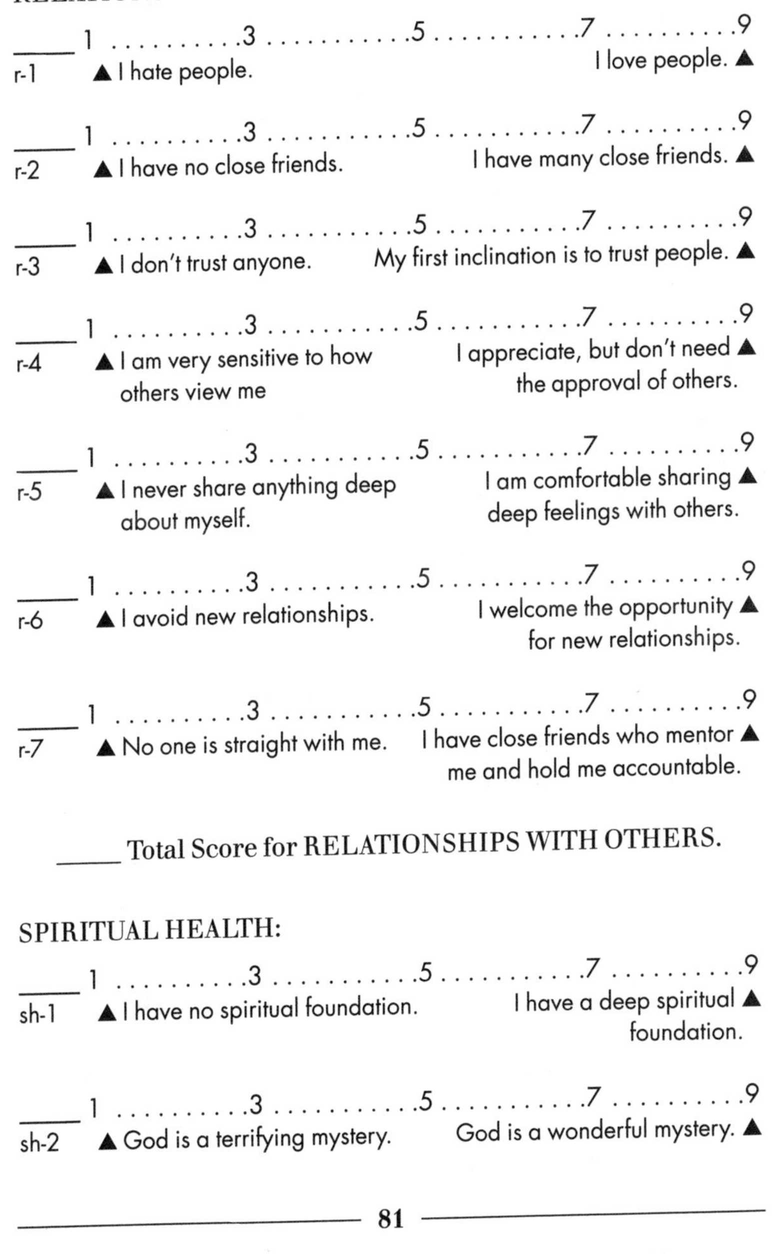

RELATIONSHIPS WITH OTHERS:

_____ 1 . . . . .3 . . . . .5 . . . . .7 9
r-1 ▲ I hate people. — I love people. ▲

_____ 1 . . . . .3 . . . . .5 . . . . .7 9
r-2 ▲ I have no close friends. — I have many close friends. ▲

_____ 1 . . . . .3 . . . . .5 . . . . .7 9
r-3 ▲ I don't trust anyone. — My first inclination is to trust people. ▲

_____ 1 . . . . .3 . . . . .5 . . . . .7 9
r-4 ▲ I am very sensitive to how others view me — I appreciate, but don't need the approval of others. ▲

_____ 1 . . . . .3 . . . . .5 . . . . .7 9
r-5 ▲ I never share anything deep about myself. — I am comfortable sharing deep feelings with others. ▲

_____ 1 . . . . .3 . . . . .5 . . . . .7 9
r-6 ▲ I avoid new relationships. — I welcome the opportunity for new relationships. ▲

_____ 1 . . . . .3 . . . . .5 . . . . .7 9
r-7 ▲ No one is straight with me. — I have close friends who mentor me and hold me accountable. ▲

_____ Total Score for RELATIONSHIPS WITH OTHERS.

SPIRITUAL HEALTH:

_____ 1 . . . . .3 . . . . .5 . . . . .7 9
sh-1 ▲ I have no spiritual foundation. — I have a deep spiritual foundation. ▲

_____ 1 . . . . .3 . . . . .5 . . . . .7 9
sh-2 ▲ God is a terrifying mystery. — God is a wonderful mystery. ▲

_____ 1 . . . . .3 . . . . .5 . . . . .7 9
sh-3 ▲ I am afraid of dying. I have no fear of death. ▲

_____ 1 . . . . .3 . . . . .5 . . . . .7 9
sh-4 ▲ God is about religion. God is about a relationship. ▲

_____ 1 . . . . .3 . . . . .5 . . . . .7 9
sh-5 ▲ I have no spiritual mentors/directors. I have spiritual people who mentor me. ▲

_____ 1 . . . . .3 . . . . .5 . . . . .7 9
sh-6 ▲ Spirituality means I *have to* give up control. Spirituality means I *can* give up control. ▲

_____ 1 . . . . .3 . . . . .5 . . . . .7 9
sh-7 ▲ I am either captive to the past or fearful of the future. I live my life in the present. ▲

_____ 1 . . . . .3 . . . . .5 . . . . .7 9
sh-8 ▲ I want to be in control. I want to be aware. ▲

_____ Total Score for SPIRITUAL HEALTH.

LIFE PURPOSE/DIRECTION:

_____ 1 . . . . .3 . . . . .5 . . . . .7 9
lpd-1 ▲ I have no road map for my life. I have a clear sense of purpose and mission for my life. ▲

_____ 1 . . . . .3 . . . . .5 . . . . .7 9
lpd-2 ▲ I have no goals for my life. I have clear goals for my life. ▲

_____ 1 . . . . .3 . . . . .5 . . . . .7 9
lpd-3 ▲ I never reflect on my life. I regularly take time for solitude and reflection. ▲

____ 1 . . . . .3 . . . . .5 . . . . .7 9

lpd-4 ▲ My life has no passion, adventure or fulfillment. — I find fulfillment in almost all my activities. ▲

____ 1 . . . . .3 . . . . .5 . . . . .7 9

lpd-5 ▲ I will do anything to avoid change. — I process change effectively and proactively. ▲

____ 1 . . . . .3 . . . . .5 . . . . .7 9

lpd-6 ▲ I feel *driven* by external forces. — I feel *called* by a Higher Power. ▲

____ 1 . . . . .3 . . . . .5 . . . . .7 9

lpd-7 ▲ I am a prisoner to urgent activities. — I always have time for the *important* over the *urgent*. ▲

____ 1 . . . . .3 . . . . .5 . . . . .7 9

lpd-8 ▲ My eulogy would not be what I want. — I am at peace with my life's accomplishments and direction. ▲

____ Total Score for LIFE PURPOSE/DIRECTION.

Whole Life Vital Signs Graph

This exercise helps you determine your "whole life vital signs" measured across ten different criteria.

First, complete the Whole Life Vital Signs Checklist, yielding a vital signs measurement for each of the ten criteria. Then, place a mark (X, O, or some other symbol) along each vertical line corresponding to the measured value for that vital sign. Note that the range of numbers varies across the different vital signs.

Remember, this is your assessment of your vital signs, today; not what others think they are or what they should be.

A positive way to view this exercise is to consider your "health" in each of these categories. Vibrant vital signs will help you if a crisis should arise in your life. Dangerously low vital signs indicate no "reserves" should a crisis arise.

	Work/Vocation	$$Money$$	Time	Physical Health	Emotional Heath	Marriage	Family Relationships	Other Relationships	Spiritual Health	Life Purpose/Direction
Vibrant	81	63	36	54	81	63	54	63	72	72
Healthy	63	49	28	42	63	49	42	49	56	56
Fair	45	35	20	30	45	35	30	35	40	40
Poor	27	21	12	18	27	21	18	21	24	24
Dangerous	9	7	4	6	9	7	6	7	8	8

For additional copies of the Whole Life Vital Signs Checklist or the Whole Life Vital Signs Graph, contact:

Jim Warner
c/o OnCourse International
2160 Meadow Avenue
Boulder, CO 80304
(303) 449-7770
(303) 449-8497

THE TRUEST YOU

Your second-half mission has been in development for a long, long time. Everything you have done—your successes and the failures—have prepared you for a second adulthood of meaning and significance. The purpose of this important step in your game plan has been to help you discover the real you—the unique person that God created you to be. As you begin to explore your options for the future, always keep this picture of who you are in mind. There is no need to reinvent or reform yourself in order to fit into a calling. The task before you is to find the calling that God has equipped you to fulfill.

That may mean setting aside those things that take you away from your truest self.

8

Find Your Spiritual Center

Whatever is at the center of our life will be the source of our security, guidance, wisdom, and power.

Stephen R. Covey

Tim Keller is a Presbyterian minister in Manhattan who presides over a large group of Baby Boomers each Sunday evening. I have not met him, but I learned about him from an article in *Forbes* written by Peggy Noonan. In a recent message, he told his upscale congregation that the thrill that comes from hearing a stirring piece of music or falling in love or watching a close basketball game is a gift from God. Like the moon's reflection of the sun's brightness, however, these things are only a reflection of something greater. The real source of that which gives us joy is God himself. All of us, says Keller, tend to worship the moon by living for art, sports, political victories, love, or whatever. Such devotion can never fulfill because we're ignoring the Source.

It is only slightly ironic that the cover of this particular issue of *Forbes* carried this headline: "Why do we feel so bad when we've got it so good?"

Although we see evidence of tremendous spiritual activity in this country—from high levels of church attendance to numerous polls showing large percentages (over ninety percent) who claim belief in God—I suspect a lot of us are worshiping the moon. That inner desire for transcendence has been temporarily fulfilled by the "reflection" of God's goodness—our work, our possessions, our leisure, our families. Unlike any previous American generation, we really do have it all, and it is not surprising that we imply a certain level of divinity from our success. But "it all" is not the true source of our joy, which is why eventually we hunger for more. As Russell Baker put it on the occasion of the seventy-fifth anniversary of the Pulitzer Prize, "There is a hunger in us for more than the money standard—for assurance that our lives have not been merely successful, but valuable—that we have accomplished something grander than just another well-heeled, loudly publicized journey from the diaper to the shroud. In short, that our lives have been consequential."

It will be difficult—I would say impossible—to make the journey from success to significance without addressing the deeper spiritual issues. Am I living only for myself? Is there a larger story, and if so, how am I a part of it? Where is God in my life? What is God doing, and where do I fit in? What is at the center of my being—emptiness or power?

It is important to note here that I am writing from my perspective as a follower of Christ with the assumption that most who read this book would at least identify themselves as sympathetic with Christian teaching, if not devout followers. As such, I believe an honest search for truth ultimately leads to Christ. At the same time, I believe the need to find your spiritual center is universal. Those of other religious persuasions or no religion at all are not exempt from this hunger for transcendence. Several years ago, Linda and I were enjoying a concert at the Lincoln Center for the Performing Arts in New York City. During the intermission, I approached a fellow concert-goer who was wearing a skull cap that Jewish people call a yarmulke and asked, "Could you explain why you wear that?" I was not trying to put him on the spot; I was just curious. He was gracious and instructive in his reply: "Jewish men wear the yarmulke to remind them there's something higher than they are."

Joseph Campbell, a brilliant researcher and writer not known for religious belief, understands this need to connect with something beyond the here and now. He describes a hero as "someone who has given his or her life to something bigger than oneself." Later, he relies on the language of faith to further explain the valiant pursuit of a nobler cause: "The literature of heroes refers to quests, risks, turning points, transformations, and ultimately to the finding of grace ...."

You do not have to be "religious" in order to be engaged in a second half of meaning and significance, and it is not my purpose here to give an apologetic for the Judeo-Christian way of thinking. But from my own observation, the very nature of significance is tied to God's larger story for mankind. The fact that some may not understand or acknowledge the connection between their agenda and God's does not invalidate either. Finding your spiritual center is really about the idea of love, which I believe most often flows from a spiritual source. Don Williams, chairman of the Trammell Crow Companies, who has realigned a big portion of his time to working in an economically deprived (yet gradually improving) section of South Dallas, says that he hasn't seen one significant effort in that neighborhood that did not come from a person of faith. I look at my own work as God's love expressed through me—as love made visible by my being involved with a movement of God himself.

Success is generally material, therefore its standards are constantly changing. The materialist answers the question "How much is enough?" with a simple but unattainable, "More." The reason you are in halftime is that you have dared to acknowledge what you sensed all along: No matter how much you gain, it is not enough. It is not that you are greedy or selfish; instead, you are seeking something that goes beyond, that lifts you into something bigger than yourself.

WHERE YOU FIT IN

All this points to the need for you to deal with the issue of your own motivation for seeking significance. What is really driving you on this journey? This step—finding your spiritual center—is tied closely to the first step, for as you disengage from your first-half activities you begin to contemplate the deeper and larger issues of your life. You begin to see how you fit into the larger story, a story that I believe begins and ends with God but has a leading role for each of us to play.

Another way of looking at this is to realize that the deeper the roots, the taller a tree can grow and the less likely it is to be toppled over by the storms that will inevitably come. In a way, there are two dimensions to such spiritual growth. One is deep-rootedness, which gives us a profound sense of purpose and endurance—what Eugene Petersen calls "long obedience in the same direction." The other is the breadth of our vision. It is vision that draws everything together. A large vision requires divine participation and leads us to be "indebted to the gifts of others," to borrow a phrase from Max DePree.

Because faith and spirituality are so personal, I cannot prescribe a list of steps that will help you find your spiritual center. I would, however, invite you to consider your current level of spiritual commitment, based on this assumption: The deeper and more personally committed you are to God, the more likely your second half will exceed your expectations.

Ponder, if you will, these important questions as a kind of warm-up for thinking about your own spiritual center:

- Are you satisfied with your beliefs, or have you always felt this was an area you would like to develop?
- Has your involvement in "religious activity" been satisfactory, or have you longed for a deeper experience of connecting with your Creator?
- Do you ever wonder why you are alive; for what purpose you were placed on earth?
- Have you noticed a change in your attitude toward religious belief as you have grown older?
- Do you ever think about the hereafter, life after death? What do you believe about this idea?
- When was the last time you prayed? What did you pray about? Why did you pray?

DRILLING DOWN

Regardless of where you are in your current relationship to things spiritual, your second-half goal is to go deeper; to establish a solid foundation of belief from which your actions will flow. Think of the athlete who is playing for the money compared to the athlete who plays because he loves the game. You've been playing for the money (or prestige or power or fame) and have begun to realize those needs can never be fully met. Your truest self needs to play for something much bigger than yourself, and I believe that is found in a relationship to God.

In my own faith there are various stages of commitment. I suspect the same is true of other faiths. After reading through the different stages below, place an "X" along the continuum to indicate where you think you are (if you are uncomfortable with the term *Christian*, insert the word that best describes your belief system).

Noncommitted Christian. Defines himself as a Christian. Believes in God, though is uncomfortable talking about it. Seldom, if ever, attends church. Unfamiliar with the Bible. A nonpracticing Christian.

Creedal Christian. At some point, usually in childhood, made a public acknowledgment of belief through confirmation or similar event. Would consider himself aligned with a denomination, but attends infrequently, usually on religious holidays such as Christmas and Easter.

Active Christian. Attends church regularly and may volunteer to serve in some capacity. May or may not have a sophisticated understanding of Christian teaching and biblical knowledge, but is generally uncomfortable or unable to articulate personal beliefs. Practice is confined within the walls of the church.

Committed Christian. Describes beliefs in terms of personal relationship with God. Has a deep spiritual life of regular praying and reading Scripture. Is usually active in a church, but does not equate church attendance or religious activities with a relationship to God. Very comfortable talking about personal beliefs and helping others learn more about his faith. Leads a life of service.

Noncommitted *Committed*

As you develop your second-half game plan, your goal is to move as far as you can toward the "committed" level. God's gift of grace to each of us requires only an open heart and honest seeking. You cannot "earn" your way into a committed relationship with God; it develops only through reflection on his teaching and, ultimately, accepting those teachings on faith.

The key concept here is inner depth and outward commitment as opposed to a belief system that is tacked onto our lives much like an accessory or optional piece of equipment that does not affect the nature of the overall package. Psychologist and author Larry Crabb has written a very useful book called *Inside Out.* From his clinical practice of over twenty years, he has found that people live their lives in an attempt to satisfy basic longings, which he puts in three categories based on their depth or superficiality. I have adapted his thinking into the four categories represented in this graphic:

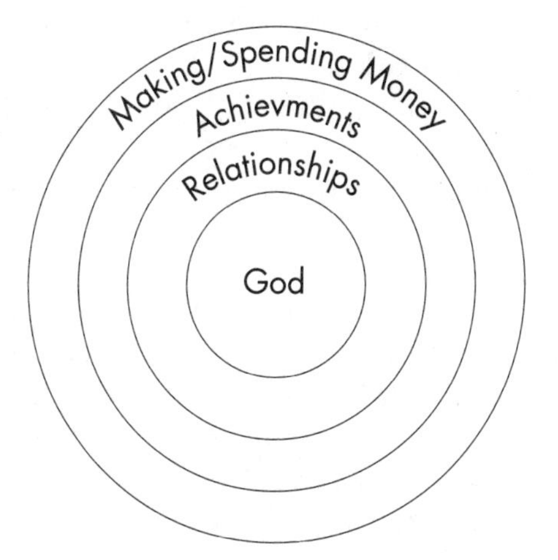

The most superficial longings are those that have to do with the making and spending of money. These longings are completely legitimate, and most of us spend the better part of our time at this level. A deeper set of longings are those that have to do with achievements—running the Boston Marathon, finishing an important project, getting elected to political office, becoming the president of your company. Closer still to the heart are those longings that can only be satisfied by close and intimate relationships—being a good father, having a satisfying marriage, cultivating intimate and enduring friendships. And at the very center are those longings that can be satisfied only by an intimate relationship with a transcendent God. These longings are a matter of existential needs that are harder to describe (bread of life, living water) and are accessible mostly by direct, personal experience.

I have found that when we face a crisis such as the one Linda and I experienced when we lost our son in 1987, it plunges us deep into the circle that has been developed the most in our lives. Some react to such crises by retreating into sensual experience and pleasures, others by losing themselves in overwork and achievement. Linda and I found that the several months after we lost Ross were a time of being inside a cocoon of close and loving relationships. For once, I was open to receiving instead of being the all-sufficient giver. It was a time when friends poured their lives into ours.

And then there is the innermost circle. I learned about this circle in a most profound way from a cancer patient named Bev Hudgins. Bev had been confined to bed for more than six months but had made an arduous and painful attempt to attend a concert. I was lucky enough to be seated next to her. I asked, "What have you learned from your experiences with cancer?" She said, "I've learned it is easy to say good-bye to all the material things. I am having a difficult time saying good-bye to those people who are closest to me. And I am so grateful that there is one relationship, my relationship with God in eternity, that I won't ever have to say good-bye to."

Here was a person who was genuinely living close to her center, and this is a kind of relationship I believe all of us can access on a daily basis without the stimulus of tragic circumstances. Unfortunately, I'm afraid the tendency of many of us is to live in the outer two circles and wonder why there is nobody there for us in a time of need.

A special word to those who have been actively involved in some form of Christian leadership, to those who attend church regularly, perhaps teach a Sunday school class or work with a ministry to the poor in your community. There is a strong temptation to interpret busyness as commitment, to assume that because you do so much good through your church or religious organization that you are deeply committed. I have found that the first-half tendency to go on autopilot is especially true for active churchgoers. My hunch is that many who read this book and placed themselves at the "committed Christian" level are, in reality, "active Christians." Maybe your second half will require *less* activity so that you can take your commitment to a deeper level.

SHARPENING YOUR FOCUS

As I learned from Mike Kami, until I determined my spiritual center—that one core principle that would singularly guide every decision I made ("what's in the box?")—I would not be able to plan strategically for the future.

In chapter 3, I asked you to begin thinking about what to put in your box. Now I would like you to begin to flesh that out a little. We have little time or opportunity to think about things like this in the first half because so much is happening, so many competing loyalties swirl around us. Halftime affords you the opportunity to sort out those competing loyalties so that you can locate the mainspring for your second-half endeavors. Look over the following list and, in the space provided, write down at least one thing you have sacrificed in order to develop or care for the individuals, things, or activities listed.

Spouse ________________________________

Children ________________________________

Career ________________________________

Health ________________________________

Hobby ________________________________

House ________________________________

Vacation ________________________________

Education ________________________________

Car ________________________________

Sports ________________________________

Community service ________________________________

Politics ________________________________

Church ________________________________

Religious beliefs ________________________________

Addictions ________________________________

Other ________________________________

Now go back over this list and try to isolate two or three categories that stand out as being the most important to you. Which ones would you *not* be willing to give up? Which ones would you die for?

________________ ________________ ________________

I suspect for many, you have narrowed your three down to these three general areas: family, religious belief, career. In order to get an honest picture of your allegiances, however, I would urge you to drill down on the career side. What is it specifically about your career that motivates you? In my case, it wasn't so much that I liked running a cable television company. I liked managing things so that my business would prosper, and the way to measure how well I managed was the bottom line. Therefore, one of the things competing for the box for me was money, symbolized by a dollar sign.

Narrowing your loyalties down to two or three as you did above helps you see your areas of priority, but it isn't enough for a second-half game plan. Eventually, you must choose one, or else your second half will be pretty much a repeat of the first. You will be easily influenced by other agendas because you have not established your own "one thing." In the following diagram, select a symbol for each of the three things you listed above and place them inside the circles.

Your goal before moving on to the next step of your game plan is to choose one of those symbols and put it in the box.

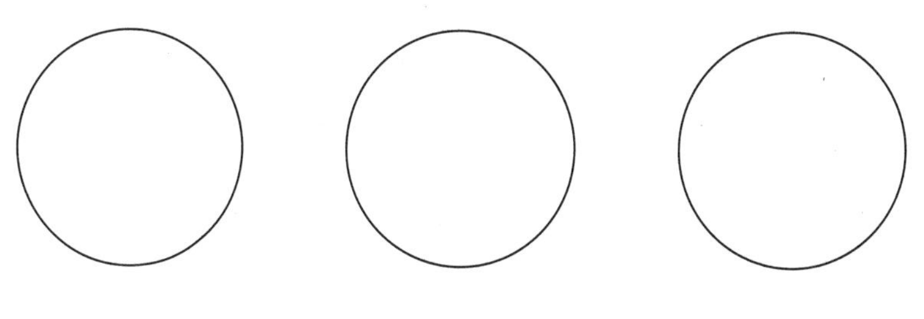

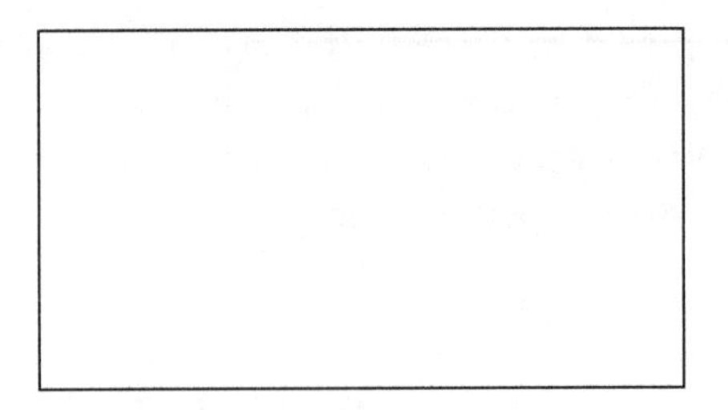

Deciding what goes in the box is a good activity to conduct on your personal retreat (chapter 6), but you may need more time to really think through the ramifications of your choice. Don't select something just because it seems to sound or look good. Select what is really the most important thing in your life—or what you genuinely want to become the most important thing in your life.

And if you truly make God the center of your life, the Bible clearly promises that those other areas that are important to you will be taken care of: "So do not worry, saying, 'What shall we eat?' or 'What shall we drink?' or 'What shall we wear?' For the pagans run after all these things, and your heavenly Father knows that you need them. But seek ye first his kingdom and his righteousness, and all these things will be given to you as well. Therefore do not worry about tomorrow, for tomorrow will worry about itself. Each day has enough trouble of its own" (Matt. 6:31–34).

9

Envision Your New Mission

> *The secret of life is to have a task, something you devote your entire life to, something you bring everything to, every minute of the day for your whole life.*
>
> **Henry Moore**

As reported in the *Wall Street Journal*, Rocky Rhodes was one of the founders of the hot, high-tech company, Silicon Graphics. Rocky read *Halftime* and among other things, it prompted him to decide it was time to rearrange his priorities. I had dinner with him when he attended a Leadership Network conference, and he told me that his first-half life had consisted of going to bed, getting up at two in the morning with software ideas, programming those into his computer, and going back to bed. He did that seven days a week, working with fierce intensity, and in the process, like many in his field, became very affluent very quickly.

As this was going on, Rocky had a Post-It note on his refrigerator that said his priorities were God, family, and work, in that order. He had pretty much settled the question of what was in the box. But one morning he looked at that Post-It again, as he had done many times before, and realized his mission did not match his priorities. He was living exactly the reverse of what he said was most important to him.

Deciding what's in the box is an important step in the journey from success to significance. But unless your mission matches your intentions, you will continue to experience dissonance that will ultimately be destructive. Your next step is to envision a new mission, one that matches whatever it is you put in the box.

Your first-half mission most likely focused on accumulation: gaining money, position, prestige, power. None of these is bad, but they cannot sustain you into the second half. The realization of this is why we are seeing so many Baby Boomers opt for early retirement—which, by the way, is not the same thing as a second-half mission. As the *Wall Street Journal* pointed out recently in an article about early retirement, "Money alone isn't enough. Baby Boomers with the freedom to quit are eager to find fulfillment outside the workplace." Most successful second halfers find that a fulfilling mission includes at least two elements: B-HAG and charity.

FIND YOUR B-HAG

By the time Mike Rawlings was thirty-seven, he had become one of the top advertising executives in the Southwest. DDB Needham Dallas is the largest group of ad agencies in Dallas and is part of DDB Needham Worldwide. For five years, Mike ran it with such skill that even his competitors had to admire him. Then, just recently, with no apparent warning, Mike did something a young CEO would never do in previous generations: he quit so that he could spend some time answering the question,

"How can I made a big difference in the next fifteen or eighteen years of my life?"

What Mike was looking for was a B-HAG (pronounced bee-hag), or a Big Hairy Audacious Goal. The concept first appeared in the best-selling book, *Built To Last: Successful Habits of Visionary Companies,* by James Collins and Jerry Porras. According to the author, major companies like Wal-Mart have survived over multiple generations because they had a B-HAG; they were able to come up with a goal so big, so impossible, and so beyond themselves that it drew the whole company into the future.

Mike Rawlings had more than surpassed his goal at DDB Needham Dallas and needed another one—something big to draw him forward into the future. As he said in an interview in the *Dallas Morning News,* "There are other mountaintops, but I think I'm going to try another range."

Your mission has to be a B-HAG—something quite ambitious with a degree of risk to it. The kind of thing that when you tell someone what you plan to do, they look at you kind of crazy and say "good luck!" The concept of B-HAG strikes at the heart of why people like underdogs and come-from-behind wins. When the odds are so big and the task so demanding, it draws you forward. It pulls the best out of you and releases energies you did not know you had.

I suppose I could have said my mission would be to help my church become a positive force for social transformation in my community, and that would have been a worthy goal. Somehow, however, that feels like something all of us ought to be doing. If you plan on adding significance to the rest of your life, your mission has to be bigger, scarier than business as usual. My stated mission is: To transform the latent energy in American Christianity into active energy. This is the bigger-than-me purpose that sustains my life. I know it is much more than I can accomplish. It is a transcendent undertaking that bonds me to others and summons my best.

As you consider your second-half mission, think big, hairy, and audacious. Go for broke. Take a look at what's in your box and then review the things you do well and enjoy doing. Start your mission quest by writing down a goal. Then multiply. At this point, don't worry if it's doable. Too many times we dream big and then kill it with a feasibility study. To really turn your second half into the adventure of a lifetime, look for a B-HAG.

CHARITY

The very first commandment God gave man in Genesis was "be fruitful and multiply." Later, in the New Testament, Jesus said that the world would recognize his followers by their fruits—by the visible results of their lives. I do not think these words were accidental, for I believe God's transcendent story for mankind has a lot to do with bearing fruit. Multiplying. Getting the most of what we have been given to work with. As Ben Franklin put it, "I want to be useful, even after my death."

The second element I have observed in those who have created a meaningful second-half mission is charity: giving away as opposed to gaining. It is the most profound paradox of the biblical teaching that you lose your life in order to gain it. For your second half to achieve significance, there must be an element of contribution to it. The saints called it "otheration." But here again, we need a new paradigm for giving. In the first half, giving was an obligation. You wrote out a check to a charity because you were pressured or shamed or emotionally arm-wrestled into making a donation. You'd be surprised how many checks are written to get rid of someone. But at the end of the year, you have no sense of making a contribution, only a slight annoyance at being hit upon so often.

To change your paradigm about giving, you really need to believe the biblical admonition that it is indeed more blessed to give than to receive. I do. In *Halftime,* I draw from what Dr. Hans Selye calls altruistic egoism, meaning the real beneficiary of your giving is you. John Marks Templeton, the legenday money manager, once remarked in a *New York Times* article, "The laws of love and charity differ from the laws of mathematics. The more you give away, the more you have left."

The first level of gain through giving is personal, but not in the sense of tax breaks or recognition from having a building named after you. The personal gain I am talking about has to do with seeing your "one thing" prosper, from knowing that the guiding principle of your life is enhanced when you give your time, energy, and resources to it.

A more eternal benefit derived from giving is found in the New Testament parable of the talents. Ultimately we will all stand before the Creator and he will ask us, "What did you do with what I gave you to work with?" That sort of levels the playing field, for whether you have a lot or little, there will be an accounting for how much of it you multiplied. In a sense, your talents, gifts, abilities, money, and mission combine to form a spiritual mutual fund. Just as you enjoy watching your financial investments grow, there is even greater joy in managing all of your spiritual assets as well.

YOUR SECOND-HALF MISSION STATEMENT

As you work through your game plan, you will eventually come up with a specific proposal for how you would like to spend your second half. Before you can do that, you need a mission statement: a clear and relatively brief declaration of why you exist and what you hope to accomplish with your life.

Peter Drucker says that everyone ought to be able to fit their mission on a T-shirt. In fact, I'm having T-shirts printed up for a lot of my friends who are social entrepreneurs:

Now, what's on *your* T-shirt?

One of the best ways to begin formulating your personal mission statement is to ask yourself some questions:

1. What do I believe?
2. What have I done uncommonly well?
3. What is my passion?
4. What needs exist in the world that I would like to meet? What do I bring to the party that others need and could benefit from?
5. What are the "should haves" that have trailed me all through the first half that I really care about?
6. How could my story and God's larger story connect?
7. In what type of activity or work do I feel most comfortable?

Two who have written extensively and well about mission statements are Stephen Covey in *The Seven Habits of Highly Effective People* and Dick Bolles in *What Color Is Your Parachute?* Covey suggests that you should focus on what you wish to be and do, based on the core values and principles that undergird your beliefs and actions (what's in the box?). Bolles added a whole section of "pink pages" in *Parachute* titled "How to Find Your Mission in Life" that combines one's religious quest with job hunting. He used the pyramid below to show the best kind of job or career is one that marries our religious beliefs or sense of mission with our work.

The Issues of the Job-Hunt

BEFORE YOU PROCEED

There's really only one way to write your personal mission statement: Just do it. The remainder of your game-plan steps builds on what you include in your mission statement; it becomes the foundation for a successful second half. In the space below, try to capture your mission in one to three sentences. Then close the book and go do something else for awhile. When you return to the book, open to this page and read your first draft of your mission statement. Before going on, think through the following questions: Is it clear? Does it indicate a direction you will take? Does it support what's in the box? Is it big enough? Does it allow you to share yourself? Does it express a deeply-held passion in your life?

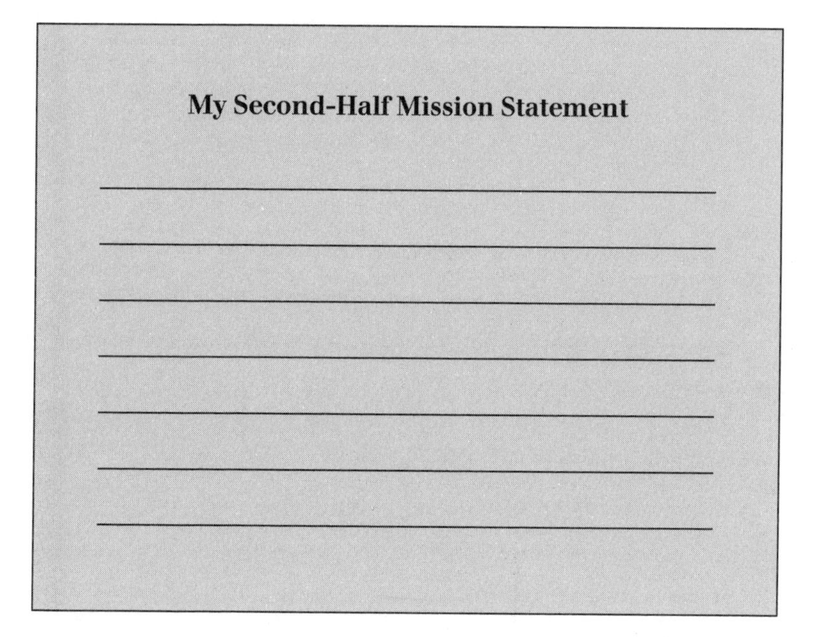
My Second-Half Mission Statement

10

Clear Your Plate

First things first and last things not at all.

Peter Drucker

In the first half, you were the all-around athlete who lettered in three sports, pulled a 3.8 GPA, and starred in the school musical. You did it all, and you did it all well.

In the second half, you will need to be more like the professional athlete. Not only will you need to select one "sport" over the others, but you will also need to focus on either offense or defense. There is nothing wrong with the other sports or the other positions, and you have already proven that you can succeed at them, so there's nothing wrong with your ability. But at this level, they are distractions. They keep you from being your best and making a significant contribution to the game.

I find it interesting that corporate giants like Proctor and Gamble, once known for its wide range of products, are now trying to focus on fewer products. In their words, they are returning to what they do best, and they feel that this will make them more profitable. In a compelling new business book titled *Focus,* Al Reis shows with an overwhelming number of case studies that in industry after industry, it's the narrowly focused companies that are the big winners, those that focus on core products and get rid of extraneous, energy-wasting ventures. Just as corporate America is rethinking its strategy of diversifying in order to grow, what I call "personal downsizing" will help keep you focused on what you do best, what you enjoy doing, and what connects with God's larger story for you.

In the second half, you need to regain control of your life by eliminating those things which distract you from your mission. This next step in your second-half game plan is a program of "planned abandonment." Look at everything that's on your plate and decide what must be cleared in order for you to make a significant contribution in the second adulthood that lies ahead of you.

WHAT'S ON YOUR PLATE?

Most people who say they are busy have no idea how busy they really are. In *The Effective Executive,* still the best book ever written on the personal side of management, Peter Drucker says we simply have no idea where our time goes until we deliberately log the specifics of our actual behavior in quarter-hour blocks. So the next thing I'm going to suggest that you do is to log your time in this manner for a seven-day period. I promise you will be shocked by all the stuff in your life. I always am. When you are done, analyze your seven-day period using the following inventory. It will become a reference point for deciding what stays and what needs to be eliminated.

Commitment Inventory

Job

Average hours per week
at your office or in the offices of others ________

Average hours per week working
on job-related projects at home ________

Average hours spent in travel
and commuting ________

Family

Average hours per week spent
alone with your spouse ________

Average hours per week spent with
children (attending concerts and sporting
events, helping with homework, etc.) ________

Community Service

Average hours per week
volunteering in your community ________

Average hours per week attending
service clubs, school committees, nonprofit
boards, charitable events, etc. ________

Church/Synagogue

Average hours per week
attending religious services ________

Average hours per week doing volunteer
work at your church or synagogue ________

Professional Development

Average hours per week in formal training
or education to enhance your career ________

Average hours per week in informal
training (reading, listening to tapes, etc.) ________

Personal Development

Average hours per week devoted to
hobbies, fitness, recreation, etc. ________

Average hours per week devoted to relaxation
(reading, watching television, etc.) ________

Total ________

1. Which of the above commitments give you the most satisfaction?
2. Which of the above feel like obligations?
3. If you had to identify one of the above in which you would like to spend more time, which would it be?
4. Is there anything from this list that you would like to eliminate completely?
5. Which of the commitments above seem to connect most closely with the real you?

In the space provided, list every board, committee, and team to which you have been assigned or are expected to regularly attend. This includes all areas of your life—business, community, church, school, etc. A good way to recall these commitments is to look back through your daily planner. When you are finished, circle those that you look forward to attending. Place an "X" in front of those you wish you could get out of.

TOO MUCH OF A GOOD THING

There's absolutely no way to know where your time goes without keeping some sort of time log. It is a very irritating thing to do because it shows you all the dribs and drabs of time you fritter away and all the interruptions you permit in your life through sheer lack of discipline or attention. Just do it. You will see.

Most people who complete an inventory like the one above discover two things. First, they realize that they really are extremely busy. Intuitively, they may have thought they were doing a lot of things, but once they quantify their commitments, they can hardly believe all they do. The reason this is such a surprise is found in their second discovery: They enjoy most of what they do. Successful people do not do very many things out of a sense of obligation but because they genuinely like getting involved in a variety of areas. If most of what you are doing are things you enjoy, it doesn't *feel* busy.

At the same time, most people who are in halftime express a common concern: There just isn't enough time for them to do all they want to do. "If I could just have twenty-five or maybe twenty-six hours each day," they say, "I could accomplish all I want to." Since twenty-four hours is all you'll ever have in a day, the obvious solution is to eliminate some things—even good things—from your plate.

The goal for this step in your game plan is to give yourself the gift of enough time so that you are not plagued with the feeling of urgency. One way you do that is through a concept developed by Bud Baab, president of Haddcom, International. He calls it e-womp, which is an acronym for "evaluating what's on my plate." It's a great tool to help people in halftime to actually create time for their second-half mission.

The goal of e-womp is to allocate enough time to what is important—to what you want your second half to be. The key to e-womp is three-fold: (1) understanding your design; (2) understanding your true self; and (3) understanding God's mission for you—your unique calling that will create your legacy.

E-womp can be a gut-wrenching experience for successful first halfers because you will need to make some tough choices about what you are going to clear off your plate. It is especially difficult if your plate is full of responsibilities and commitments that "fit" your unique design—that embody your truest self. Here again, think of the young high school athlete who lettered in several sports. As he considers a collegiate athletic career, he realizes he needs to select one sport, knowing that to compete at the college level, he will have to focus all his energies on that sport. If he is good enough to attract the attention of the pros, he will have to specialize even more.

Linda and I have benefited enormously from the window on the world which the Young Presidents' Organization (YPO) has provided us. Of the several hundred YPO presentations we have heard, none stuck with me more than one I heard at the Waldorf Astoria years ago by a man named Norman Cohn. The Norman Cohn Trust takes over distressed businesses from their lenders, making enormous returns from turning them around. His lecture was titled "How to Keep Your Company Out of the Hands of Norman Cohn Trust."

Cohn said that every company that falls into trouble demonstrates a common pattern. The managers are successful in operating in a single, focused area (let's say shoe stores). Lenders come along and offer them capital to expand because they are such great retailers. The shoe store operators go out and buy a chain of, let's say, drug stores—still retailing, but not quite the same expertise. Soon the drug stores get in trouble, and the managers divert their energy to rescuing them. The shoe stores then falter from lack of focus and attention. Now both businesses are in trouble. The bank calls its loan in and calls Norman. He meets with the company and says, "I'm buying your company. You will still be the managers. Within twenty-four hours you will decide to sell either the shoe stores or the drugstores, and from then on I will give you twenty-five percent of the gain in profits."

Cohn went on to say that the managers *always* go back to focusing on what they did best. All but one of his twenty-seven acquisitions resulted in success for him and the original managers, all because of focus.

In your first half, you did a lot of things well. Now you need to limit yourself to only a few things to which you will devote your time and energy—activities that will allow you to pursue your second-half mission. There are too many good causes and profitable activities for you to commit to in this life. If you keep trying to do them all, you will eventually grow less and less effective in each endeavor. It's what Peter Drucker calls "frittering yourself away."

People who are Christians have an especially difficult time staying focused because they are so susceptible to pleas for help. Any visible Christian businessman can count on being asked to serve on at least three or four boards, but he often ends up doing what God called *them* to do, not what God called *him* to do. In my work with churches and church leaders, I have discovered that many Christians are working very hard at things that do not fit their skills, abilities, and interests. One way to counter this is to say no to anything that doesn't maximize these areas in your life, even though it is only five or ten degrees off your mission.

You have already begun thinking about your commitments and responsibilities. Now go back to your commitment inventory and begin prioritizing them. For any activity that will be effective in helping you pursue your second-half mission, place the initials 2H, for second half. For any activity that will be *least* effective in your second-half mission, draw a line through it. In other words, identify those commitments and responsibilities that need to be eliminated so that you have enough time and energy to focus on your second-half mission.

RENEGOTIATING RELATIONSHIPS

I've watched a number of people go through the e-womp process, and almost always it requires some renegotiations in the relationships they have developed throughout their first halves. Hard-charging executives who have let their relationship with their spouses slip on the priority scale, for instance, realize that a fully-functional partnership is pivotal to a dynamic and meaningful second half. If you have conditioned your spouse to be a silent, inactive partner, you will definitely need to explain your new priorities and be open to your spouse's concerns. Don't make the mistake of assuming that because you now want to shift from success to significance, your spouse will automatically approve. You may have conditioned him or her to expect a certain lifestyle and standard of living. To suddenly start talking about significance, mission, calling, and your true self might invite a reaction somewhat different from the one you are expecting.

My partner in the Leadership Network for twelve years, Fred Smith, is a good example. He came to a point where he could see the demands of travel brought on by the upcoming plans for our organization would conflict with his desire to spend time with his two daughters, ages eleven and sixteen. The way he put it in a letter to those we serve was, "I've spent a good portion of the last twelve years with wonderful and stimulating people . . . a thousand miles from home."

Fred's decision to stay closer to home evolved over several years and was a decision that affected and involved each member of his family. Don't assume that a change—even one that makes you more accessible to your family—can be made without their input.

This is much more than "touchy-feely" stuff. It is what I call "family ecology," the notion that if one member of the family changes, the whole family must change. Halftime is a monumental change in the life of an adult. Have you discussed it with your spouse? Your children? What are the implications of these changes on them?

You may also need to renegotiate your relationship with your employer. This can be tricky and more than a little risky. One forty-three-year-old man I know decided to renegotiate his role as the president of a multimillion-dollar conglomerate by asking for a less demanding position. Unheard of in American business, his board nonetheless granted his request. As you can imagine, this involved a lifestyle change (he took a pretty significant cut in salary), but he is convinced this was a choice that had to be made in order to free him up for a second half where he could focus on his agenda, not someone else's. It's about what you want to do with your life.

I will be the first to admit that a president of a multimillion-dollar corporation is in a better position to reduce his involvement than a midlevel manager. On the other hand, we all tend to live just a little higher than we need to, so regardless of one's position, a reduction in income is many times an option to consider when the benefit is regaining control of your life.

I am not suggesting you quit your job or take a lesser position in order to have a second half that is better than the first. But to be honest, changes like this are not uncommon as men and women try to clear things from their plates that do not contribute to their calling, things that do not fit their true selves. There are a lot of affluent people selling insurance or running businesses who are trying to cope with the dissonance between who they are and what they are doing. Sometimes, to align who you are with what you are doing, you need to do something different. This important step in your game plan may show you that you need to make some changes in how you allocate your time.

As you begin looking at ways to clear your plate, it will be helpful (and realistic!) to keep the following questions before you:

1. What level of income do I need to maintain my standard of living?
2. Is downward mobility an option? How much of a reduction in income could I take and still maintain my standard of living?
3. What changes could I comfortably make in my lifestyle in order to trade a lower income for more time and less stress?
4. How long could I manage if I took an unpaid leave of absence from my current job?
5. Is there a way I can combine those things I really enjoy with God's bigger story in such a way that I can still earn a decent income?
6. Can I renegotiate my deal with my company to work less than full-time? What is the contribution my company values most from me?

SAYING NO TO OPA

Frequently seen bumper sticker: Just Say No!

What you are doing in this step of your game plan—clearing your plate—means often saying no to other people's agendas (OPA). You are declaring your allegiance to what's in the box and, in the process, regaining control of your life. I have asked you to look at the more drastic ways this can be done, but sometimes it's just a matter of better time management and more effective delegating. I know several men who are fully engaged in second-half missions who have not changed their employment picture. They have learned that by the time you're in your fourth or fifth decade, you can effectively turn a fifty-hour-per-week job into one that takes you only twenty-five or thirty.

When you combine a smarter use of your office time with the elimination of everything on your plate that does not effectively advance your second-half mission, you will have plenty of time left over to pursue *your* agenda. You work smarter, not harder or longer.

In Al Ries' book, *Focus,* the introduction begins with these lines: "The sun is a powerful source of energy. Every hour the sun washes the earth with billions of kilowatts of energy. Yet with a hat and some sun screen, you can bathe in the light of the sun for hours at a time with few ill effects. A laser is a weak source of energy. A laser takes a few watts of energy and focuses them in a coherent stream of light. But with a laser, you can drill a hole in a diamond or wipe out a cancer." It's all about focus.

The next step in your game plan is to make sure you build a team for your second half.

11

Build a Second-Half Team

We all live spiritually by what others have given us in the significant hours of our life.

Albert Schweitzer

Two are better than one . . . for if either of them falls the one will lift up his companion. But woe to the one who falls when there is not another to lift him up . . . and if one can overpower him who is alone, two can resist him. A cord of three strands is not quickly torn apart.

The book of Ecclesiastes

Americans are the most individualistic people in the world. We love our independence and believe that, for the most part, our success is largely the work of our own hands. That's not to say we don't give credit along the way to those who have helped us or that we never work in teams. But in the really big things—the things that matter most—we like to call the shots and not have to deal with what others think about our decisions.

That won't work in the second half because your goal—meaning and significance—is so much bigger than you are. The underlying concept is simple: The combined wisdom and diverse gifts of a group are an invaluable resource. Here again, the model of Jesus is instructive. When it came time for Jesus to begin his one thing—his mission on earth—he formed a team, choosing twelve men from diverse backgrounds to go with him on the journey. And among the twelve, he chose three, you might say an Office of the President, to work especially close with him.

There's too much at stake in your second half to go into something ill-advised and untested by others. I'm as headstrong and independent as anyone, but I have learned not to fully trust my ideas until I've had a chance to hear from close friends and associates whom I trust. Whether they critique or affirm, or just encourage me in the direction I'm heading, their input is invaluable. These are people with whom I feel comfortable and who I can trust to be honest with me. They form a safe haven where I can think my confusion out loud, share my fears and concerns, unload my pain, and celebrate my successes. I have found this concept to be so valuable that I now have three or four teams to consult with in the different areas of my life before I start things.

You may have worked with teams at the office, but your second-half team is different. At work, you are generally assigned to a team and told to combine everyone's skills and knowledge in order to solve a business problem or create a new idea. Again, you were working on someone else's agenda, with people you did not choose, to solve a problem that wasn't yours. Your second-half team will be one of your own choosing. This requires some careful thinking. Who do you select, how do you get them to join your team, and what do you do once you've built your team?

FINDING WORLD-CLASS TEAMMATES

How do you decide who to invite onto your team? The primary qualifications should be honesty and trust. You want people who will be strong enough to give you the truth and impeccable in their ability to keep confidences. Most of your teammates should be close to your own age group, having a sense of what you are going through as a halftimer who's at a crucial juncture in life. Your team will be strengthened if you seek some variety in terms of politics, perspectives, personalities, and net worths. In other words, don't build a team made up of your clones. There is no magic number as to the size of your team, but I would recommend no fewer than three and no more than six. And you should select people who know you well and who respect you for who you are (rather than what you do, how successful you've been, or how much money you've earned).

One word of caution. In most professions there is a "good old boy" network built pretty much along the lines of "I'll scratch your back if you scratch mine." There is nothing wrong with this kind of networking, but generally these aren't the people you want on your team. Those relationships seldom get very deep beneath the surface and tend to carry with them expectations and obligations. You want teammates who will be strong enough to tell you the truth and compassionate enough to encourage and comfort you.

My friend Ken Blanchard, author of the best-selling *One Minute Manager*, has learned a lot about building an effective team. His successful training and development business has thirty-five partners around the world. He says there are two aspects to partnerships—essence and form. Essence has to do with having compatible values while form has to do with the nuts and bolts of working together. "Once we find a partner with whom we feel we have essence, we have found that form often takes care of itself," Ken says.

Below, list as many names as possible of people you know who share your core set of values and will be honest with you:

Before you approach the people on this list, think through what it is you will be asking them to do. From my experience, there are two minimum requirements for effective teammates: (1) commitment to at least one year of regular feedback and input to your second-half plans, and (2) availability to meet at least quarterly, though monthly would be better. Keep in mind that if your teammates are scattered geographically, you can meet via conference call. However, I would try to select people who could meet with you in person at least a couple of times during the year.

The rest is pretty simple and straightforward. Take a prospective teammate out to lunch, tell him you're about to embark on a journey that could lead to some changes in your life and that you'd like him to join a few others in regularly giving feedback to your plans as they develop. You might offer to provide the same kind of feedback for him. When you have enough teammates to suit you, there's only one thing left to do: call a meeting!

STILL NOT CONVINCED?

There's very little I do without first running it by a few trusted friends, but I realize that not everyone is wired the way I am. So if the idea of choosing a team and meeting regularly seems unnecessary or makes you uncomfortable, there are other ways to make sure your ideas and plans have the benefit of objective criticism.

Some people look for a team that has already been formed and join it. The team, in this case, is usually an organization dedicated to a goal similar to your second-half mission. For example, several years ago a publishing executive decided he would be more fulfilled using his administrative and leadership gifts in the nonprofit sector. He remembered an acquaintance who was on the board of an inner-city mission and made a phone call. A few months later he joined their team as executive director and gave them several years of world-class leadership.

The point of this example is that this man did not go off on his own and try to negotiate his second half. By joining the organization, he had a ready-made team that included a staff and an independent board of directors. Any new idea or dream he wanted to implement was automatically given the benefit of shared wisdom and honest, constructive criticism.

Another way to build a second-half team is to start your own organization, which in a way is what I've done through Leadership Network. I first went to a few trusted friends and told them of my desire to devote the second half of my life to something that connected my own story (experiences, skills, gifts, etc.) with God's transcendent story. In the back of my mind I was thinking seminary, pastor, maybe missionary. Fortunately, my friends' honest response directed me to start something brand new. Fred Smith and I began Leadership Network as "two guys and a typewriter." Fred's partnership was pivotal: no Fred Smith, no Leadership Network!

If you decide to form a team by starting your own organization, be wary of the temptation to turn it into your own personal kingdom. In other words, find people who care about you, who are honest, and who will be strong enough to tell you the truth, even if you are the boss.

Before we leave this concept of finding a team, I should mention that the big movement in larger churches is the small group. These are groups of generally eight to ten persons—often organized around mutual interests—that meet regularly to talk about things important to them, study a book or the Bible, and pray. If you do not feel comfortable selecting a few individuals to be a part of your second-half team, and if you attend a church that offers such small groups, you should at least consider joining one.

FIND A MENTOR

Finally, I believe everyone in the second half should have a mentor—someone at least twenty years older than you who can become a de facto member of your team. I have been blessed to be able to regularly tap into the wisdom of organizational and social change expert Peter Drucker. I cannot think of anything I have done in my second half without first consulting with Peter (and there are many things I haven't done because I heeded Peter's advice). It helps to talk with someone who has already traveled the pathway of the journey before you.

A close friend of mine who is fully into his second half recommends two to four mentors at a time, cycling them every three to five years. He says he is always looking for new mentors. Not bad advice. Demographers tell us there is no shortage of retired persons to whom we could look for a mentoring relationship. My hunch is that most of these people left the scene too early and with plenty of savvy to share.

Now that you have a team, it's time to make some serious steps into the second half. It's almost time to jump off the diving board, but not quite.

12

Test Your Way In

Suppose one of you wants to build a tower. Will he not first sit down and estimate the cost to see if he has enough to complete it? For if he lays the foundation and is not able to finish it, everyone who sees it will ridicule him, saying, "This fellow began to build and was not able to finish."

Luke 14:28–30

At this stage in your journey from success to significance, you should be starting to envision a specific second-half mission. What are the possibilities? What options are realistically open to you? If you could design the perfect situation that would maximize your gifts and interests with your desire to give something back to society, what would it look like? In other words, how are you beginning to answer the question, "What are you going to do about what you believe?"

While halftime is that interval in which you ponder this tantalizing issue of significance and meaning, you can't stay there forever. There comes a time when we need to turn the dream into a reality, and that time is approaching.

The next step in your game plan is to actually test the waters before you dive.

Which of the following options are viable for you?

- Continue in my present job
- Change my present job description
- Change jobs but stay in my present career field
- Change to a new career
- Pursue a double track in parallel careers
- Seek additional training or education
- Retire early with adequate annual income

Now try to be very specific about how you would like to spend your second half. I have found that the best way to do this is to get a description of your second-half destination down on paper. Marge Blanchard likes to suggest that you write out the script for a "Fantasy Day" some time in the future. Include things such as the goals you hope to achieve, how you spend your time, where you will be located (home, separate organization, etc.), who you would like to be with, how you will feel about what you are doing, and other resources you will need. Visualize a wonderful day in the future with as much imagination and concrete detail as you can picture in your mind.

SEISMIC TESTING

This is a great way to minimize risks. It's a concept borrowed from the oil business that I first discussed in *Halftime*, and it involves doing some geological testing instead of just setting up an expensive rig and starting to drill. The idea is that you shoot at a subsurface formation from many different points and the configuration of what's beneath the surface begins to emerge.

The key to seismic testing for the second half is listening. I have found that by asking six or seven different smart people about an issue I am working on, a pattern begins to emerge based on the different points of view I wouldn't have seen in looking from my single vantage point. Sounds obvious, I know, but I am amazed at the number of people who dream up a second-half mission and launch it before they've talked to anyone about it. As you come up with ideas for a second-half mission, test them on your team or with others who are doing similar work.

LOW-COST PROBES

Another way to test the waters before diving in is to conduct some low-cost probes. For something to qualify as a low-cost probe it shouldn't cost much; it should be well-defined; it should involve only a limited time commitment; and it should offer hands-on experience. If you're considering a career change, for example, spend a day shadowing someone in that field. If you're thinking of some type of overseas service, take a short-term volunteer missions trip. Organizations like Youth with a Mission, International Aid, World Vision, and others make this possible.

Michael Crichton, the novelist who gave us *Jurassic Park* and *Rising Sun,* which have helped him make the Forbes Top Forty Entertainers List, began his career as a doctor. He notes that a lot of people go to medical school without ever understanding the daily work of a doctor. He describes an exercise that is done during the first week of medical school where students are asked to dissect a corpse. The first surgery is to cut the skull in half with an electrical surgical saw. When confronted with the "real thing," Crichton observed that not a few med students decided that a life in medicine wasn't for them after all. He was one of them. This is perhaps an extreme example of what I mean by a low-cost probe, but don't commit your second half to medicine until you've cut the skull.

If your particular second-half mission would benefit from a low-cost probe, list three organizations or businesses with whom you might be able to arrange one:

1.

2.

3.

PARALLEL CAREER

As I pointed out earlier, don't think you are in your current position by accident. If you have been successful, it is because you are uniquely qualified to be doing what you're doing; you have the temperament, the inherent gifts, and the education. There is a good chance that your second-half mission will build on these good foundations. In fact, most second halfers I know are doing their "one thing" alongside their current first-half work.

More and more, it looks like we will experience a series of different careers as we go through life. The best way to understand this development is to look at a career as an "S" curve. The old paradigm—the one your father or grandfather may have experienced—looks like this:

The "S" Curve

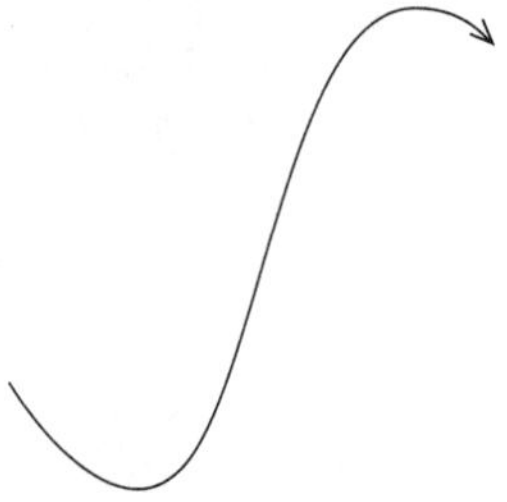

You get a job, climb the ladder, reach a peak level of effectiveness, and then hold on until retirement. If you really didn't feel like retiring, you might have tried extending your career:

The Career Extender

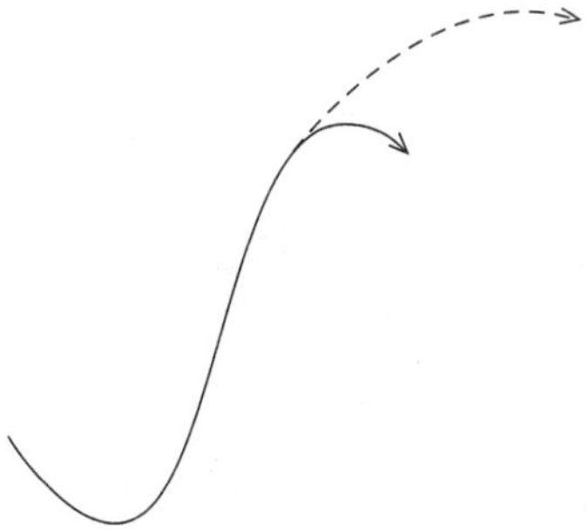

The new paradigm—one that is becoming more and more available to today's Boom generation—involves a series of "S" curves that represent career changes:

The Career Changer

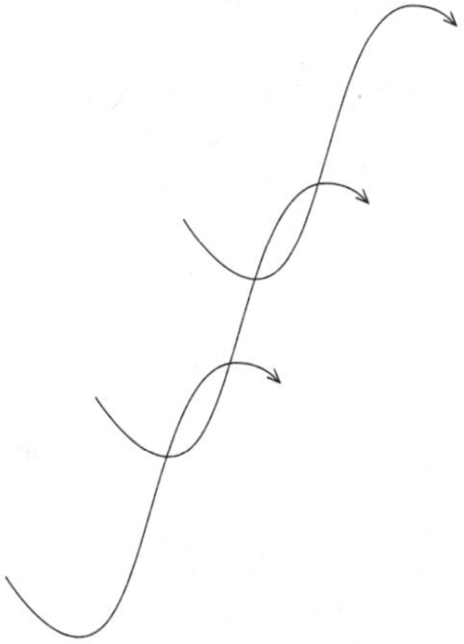

In this model, a person may move from one career to another several times. A variation on this is what we call the parallel career, where the second-half career may be lived out alongside your primary career. Eventually, but not always necessarily, the second-half career beomes the primary career as you decide to leave your initial job entirely. The parallel career looks like this:

The Parallel Career

I am endebted to Charles Handy in *The Age of Paradox* for stimulating my thinking about s-curves, and to Pat McMillan of Team Resources in Atlanta for help in working out the implications of s-curves for second halfers. With their help I have come up with what I call "The Development Phases for a Significant Second Half":

The Development Phases for a Significant Second Half

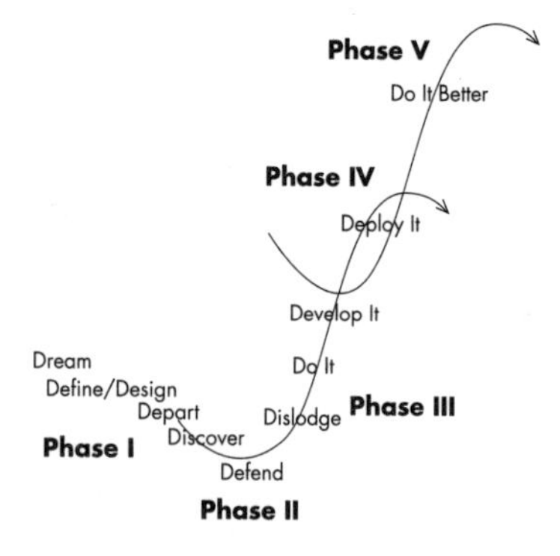

Looks good on paper, but does it really work? Not long ago I sat at dinner with Elmer Johnson, who was general counsel at General Motors. He now is with the Chicago law firm of Kirkland and Ellis. Elmer is what they call in the trade a "rainmaker." He really enjoys the law firm and has made a deal with his partners to work part time on a fixed fee, allowing him to pursue other activities in parallel that he would not have the time or energy to do if he was putting in the usual sixty-hour weeks. He looked like a happy man to me.

As I pointed out in an earlier chapter, after you've spent ten to fifteen years in a particular field, you've developed efficiencies that allow you to do your job at half-speed. You accomplish in twenty hours what used to take you forty. Your employer may be willing to renegotiate your work arrangement to allow you to be involved in some form of service to your community. If you like your first-half line of work and you need a regular income, this is a great option for easing into your second half.

WADING IN VS. DIVING IN

This is really a combination of the three previous ways of testing your second-half mission. Let's say you are an insurance agent and your life mission is to help at-risk kids. To make that happen, you would eventually like to start an organization like the "I Have a Dream Foundation" that mentors kids from difficult neighborhoods.

You run this wild dream past several people who have done this sort of work and get some valuable input (seismic testing). You are still in your first-half work, so there is limited risk. You are encouraged to go ahead, and as you do you feel that working with at-risk kids matches your skills and passions. So you wade in a little further by deciding to volunteer in an already established inner-city ministry (low-cost probe). This experience further confirms the validity of your mission, so you head for deeper waters.

You have already begun to clear your plate, and you can see financial freedom in three or four years if you play your cards right. But for now, you still need to work three days a week in your first-half career. You decide to volunteer one day per week in the inner-city mission and to spend another day planning and making contacts to see what the funding and staffing requirements would be to set up an "I Have a Dream" chapter in your city.

Over the next two years, you gradually cut back on your office hours as you transfer your business over to other partners and younger proteges in order to increase the time you devote to your mission. Eventually, you reach the point where you can spend eighty percent of your time on your second-half dream. In this way, you are working on a parallel career that will become your second-half career.

Very likely, your dream will not come true for another few years, but when it does, you will be fully in the second half—fully engaged in something that connects your true self with what you believe God has all along been preparing you to do. You will have moved from success to significance, connecting to the larger story.

EIGHT ALTERNATIVES

There is no single route to second-half significance, no formula that always works for every person. Instead, there are multiple pathways that could be a part of your overall journey.

Here are eight ways to pursue significance in the second half of your life. Use the scales to evaluate the extent to which you are pursuing each alternative, with "1" representing no involvement, and "5" representing high involvement.

Eight Paths to Second-Half Significance

	Not at all involved		Somewhat involved		Highly involved
Volunteering You donate substantial time and energy to a cause you deem significant.	1	2	3	4	5
Being a donor You contribute financial resources to a cause you deem significant.	1	2	3	4	5
Using your business as ministry You use your enterprise to accomplish kingdom work even as you pursue your core business. (You may also designate profits toward one of the other alternatives.)	1	2	3	4	5
Becoming a board member You provide leadership and expertise to a nonprofit organization that has a mission you deem significant.	1	2	3	4	5
Partnering You team up with someone involved full-time in a cause you deem significant, acting as a silent partner to provide resources to that individual in whatever ways are needed to accomplish meaningful results.	1	2	3	4	5
Establishing a parallel career You take on an executive responsibility for a cause you deem significant, even as you continue to carry out your vocational commitments.	1	2	3	4	5
Becoming an organizational leader You make a fundamental career change by becoming the executive of an established organization that has a mission you deem significant.	1	2	3	4	5

Becoming a social entrepreneur	1	2	3	4	5
You use your entrepreneurial expertise and experience to start and build a nonprofit initiative designed to meet a societal need in an innovative way.					

Each of these options can be pursued in either foolish ways or intelligent ways. The challenge of people wanting to make a difference is to be smart about the nature of their involvement—at whatever level it happens to be.

Two final comments about testing your way into the second half. First, be patient in your testing. Listen to the results and make adjustments to your plans. You spent four years in college and then more in preparation for your first-half career. It may take at least that long to move from halftime to the second half. On the other hand, if all you do is test, you're basically dabbling and will not make much progress toward your ultimate goal.

At some point you need to take a deep breath, hold your nose, and jump.

13

Reparadigm Your Life

What we do know, however, is that this transformation of our lifetimes is really taking place.... It is real. And what it means is that you may live a great deal longer than you expect.... If you have had reasonably good health habits, by the time you celebrate your sixtieth birthday, instead of being on the downward slope of old age you may have two or three decades of productive adult time ahead of you .... If you are not aware of this trend, you may make decisions that essentially foreshorten your own opportunities. You could reach fifty and think your most creative or productive years are behind you (they aren't); or you could think that you'll be old at sixty-five (you probably won't be).

Lydia Bronte in *The Longevity Factor*

I had hoped to write an entire book without using the word *paradigm*, but I would have had to eliminate this important step. Basically, a paradigm is a particular way of looking at things. I've turned this heavily exploited noun into a verb to suggest you need to change the way you look at a lot of things if you want your second half to be significantly better than the first.

In other words, you cannot view the second half through your first-half glasses. Here are a few areas in which a new point of view will be especially important for your second adulthood.

AGE

Betty Friedan learned something that most people who work in nursing homes have known for years: Being old is not the same as acting old. Her landmark book, *The Fountain of Age,* is a fascinating account of her research into the aging process. Among other things, she concluded that the mind plays an important role in how we age. The way we view ourselves—and the way we allow others to view us—she suggests, determines whether we are growing older or "vitally age." And according to her research, the existing and almost universally held paradigm for aging is a period of decline and decay. Among other sources, she cites a Louis Harris Poll done in 1975 and repeated in 1981 in which the majority of young and middle aged respondents viewed those over sixty-five as having "very serious problems," and described them as "lonely, unhealthy, poor, and fearful." In that same study, respondents over sixty-five also thought at least half of their peers had "very serious problems" in those areas. As Friedan observes, "Myth has replaced reality."

I'm sure you have seen people who are vitally aging. They are obviously not twenty-five-year-olds, but they act a lot more like twenty-five-year-olds than fifty-year-olds. These are the people who run marathons in their sixties, read *Wired* magazine instead of *Modern Retirement,* and refuse to see themselves as "senior citizens."

The person who is merely aging is a fifty-five-year-old who tries to look like a twenty-year-old. The person who is vitally aging doesn't mind looking fifty, but can talk comfortably with a twenty-year-old. The aging male likes his "oldies" station and tries to recreate the past. The vitally-aging male likes the older music too, but listens and tries to understand a variety of new music styles. (Sir George Solti left the Cleveland Symphony after twenty years because he wanted to conduct more modern music.) Aging people talk about yesterday; vitally-aging people talk about tomorrow.

Those who approach the end of the first half usually have two tendencies when it comes to age: mourn the passage of time or deny it. Neither response is helpful to your second-half adventure. Instead, you need to adopt a brand-new way of looking at your age: accept the chronology but reject the psychology. In other words, accept how old you are, but refuse to let it affect your outlook on life.

Over lunch one day, Jim Sundberg, former catcher for the Texas Rangers, told me that most professional athletes are in denial over the imminent end of their careers (he said the average baseball player has about five years in the majors). They're never ready when the end comes because they haven't prepared for it. According to Sundberg, sixty percent of baseball players get a divorce within the first few years after their major league careers end.

There is no single, bulletproof technique or method for changing your age paradigm, but there are some things you can consciously try that will help you make the transition from aging to vitally aging:

First, "down age" yourself by thinking ten years younger than you are. You don't need to force things here. Because of better health habits and increased longevity, today's sixty-year-old generally feels, looks, and does the same as yesterday's fifty-year-old. This isn't necessarily about psyching yourself up, but is a reality of the 1990s that you need to claim for yourself. Jacqueline Kennedy Onassis provided us with a beautiful example of life at sixty. Cher is fifty. The Rolling Stones are still rocking... and rolling. *People* magazine recently named Sean Connery "The Sexiest Man Alive." It's not the way it used to be.

Second, emulate older models rather than younger ones. Even as you think ten years younger than you are, look for vitally aging men twenty-five years your senior who are active, vibrant, and engaged. Get to know them. Hang out with them if you can. Their enthusiasm and zest for living can be contagious. Their lives demonstrate what is possible. Peter Drucker always has this effect on me.

Third, banish retirement from your thinking. There is absolutely nothing about retirement in the Bible. It's a modern invention, and social economists are suggesting it may already be obsolete, an impossibility in the next decade. So get ahead of the curve and refuse to think about and plan for retirement. I think retirement is a bad idea anyway. In my mid-forties, I established as one of my goals "to be a productive seventy-year-old." One of my friends who is retired described the retirement experience as one of "having five Saturdays a week." He was constantly trying to find ways to fill his time. As you approach your seventies, you may need to change the pace of your work or the nature of your work, but if you've got a good second-half thing going, why stop at a certain age?

Fourth, quit thinking of anyone past fifty as over the hill. Again, if you allow yourself to think of the second half of your life as being in decline, you will begin to decline. "As a man thinketh, so is he," says a wise proverb.

Fifth, read, listen, and watch those who are young. I think it's important to stay in touch with trends. It keeps you on the edge. Most media is targeted to certain demographics, and a good way to maintain an adventurous, youthful outlook is to regularly read magazines, listen to music, and watch television and movies that are aimed at the generation immediately behind you.

And finally, fight age tracking. Most churches and social organizations offer activities for segments of their congregation based on age. I understand the thinking behind it from the organizer's perspective, but it sure reinforces the idea that you aren't what you used to be. Break the mold and visit a "couples with young children" class at your church. It will help you think young, and you will be a valuable resource to all those couples wondering if they will ever survive the diaper years.

Peter Drucker, in a *Boardroom Reports* article, recommends other options to help you avoid the aging-as-decline mentality: double-track (or even triple-track) in parallel careers; turn a hobby into a profession; start all over again in a new career; and work well past retirement age. "The time to think about new avenues of useful activity is not when you're 55 or 60 but when you're 40 or 45," Drucker says. "Chances are, if you haven't learned a way to reinvigorate your productiveness by age 50, you never will."

To reparadigm your concept of age, you basically need to correct the idea that young is good, old is bad. To the adage, "you're only as old as you feel," I would add, "and you're only as old as you think."

IDENTITY

The first-half paradigm for identity is external—we define ourselves chiefly by our work, our possessions, our busyness, even our children. For the second half, seek to identify yourself by internal standards: your character, your values, your beliefs, your contribution, your mission.

Your second-half identity may be your capacity to love others and make that love visible in your actions.

How do you set about creating a second-half identity? Part of this is addressed in previous steps where you eliminate those things from your life that do not contribute toward your mission. You limit your commitments, find more time to think, focus in on your "one thing," and commit it to the box. You learn to "just say no!"

But there is another area of elimination I have not already mentioned that deserves special attention: possessions. I am convinced that many people never make it to a life of significance because they are trapped in a lifestyle that won't let them. They are mortgaged to the hilt and cannot see anything in the second half but more hard work to pay for everything they have accumulated. Add to that reality the fact that their identities are wrapped up in their lifestyle and you can see why retirement looks so good: finally they can slow down, disappear off the social radar screen, and downsize in a conventional manner.

Why wait until you retire if you can shed some baggage that you accumulated during the first half? Most people I know who have a garageful of toys never have the time to use them. The boat, the RV, the country club membership, and the house in Vail really function as status, which is another way of saying they provide you with your identity.

Are possessions bad? No, but realize they can get in the way. Ask yourself, "If I got rid of ________, would I still be me?" If the answer is yes, keep the boat and enjoy it. If the answer is no, get rid of the boat and anything else that's getting between you and your true self.

TIME

The third candidate for a new paradigm is your understanding of time. In the first half, time is a precious commodity that must always be used productively. Time is still precious in the second half, but it is to be enjoyed and savored as much as it is to be used. Time is an enemy in the first half; it should become a friend in the second.

In a review of the novel *Slowness,* by Leland Kendera, the reviewer notes that lives lived frantically are more intensely forgotten than lives lived slowly. The novelist intimates, says the reviewer, that people are grasping for the "oblivion of speed.... The author presents them as contemporary dancers who live more for show than for substance."

Not long ago, on a flight to Washington D.C., my seatmate was Kay Bailey Hutchinson, our senator here in Texas. All the way to her seat, a staff person was briefing her. During the flight, half the people in the first-class cabin lobbied her. Even as she listened, she was going through a stack of papers, marking notes on most of them. And the minute the plane landed, another staff person began briefing her. I told her that I thought the most thoughtful thing I could do was to keep my mouth shut, and she graciously agreed. The one question I did ask was, "Are you enjoying being a United States senator?" "Not yet," she said.

What a way to live.

The second half is about substance, so it stands to reason we need to not only lighten up the load of our possessions, but we should slow down as well so that we can hear our lives speaking to us again. People who don't have time to reflect often get derailed. Several years ago, Senator David Durenburger told me that senators have no time for reflection. That explains a lot, doesn't it?

As you craft your second-half adventure, try to break out of the eight-hour day, forty-hour week paradigm. An effective program known as Strategic Coaching recommends a schedule I think is perfect for the second half. You basically allocate one-third of your days to "focus days" for highly productive, intense activity; one-third to "buffer days" (cleaning up messes, preparing for focus days, tending to correspondence, administration, etc.), and one-third to "free days" for thinking and reflection. The participants I know tell me that in following this schedule they lead richer lives and are more productive than their prior frantic lives allowed.

The late Henri Nouwen offered a slightly different approach to dividing your time into three stages: solitude at night, community in the morning, and ministry in the afternoon. Again, the point is not so much a legalistic approach to time management, but making sure there is balance in your life.

Changing a paradigm is not unlike a football player being traded. While Deion Sanders played for the Forty-Niners, he viewed Dallas as the enemy. Now that he's a Cowboy, he has a different view of Dallas *and* of San Francisco. Nothing has really changed about either team. What changed was how Deion looked at them. (Albeit he had a pretty good incentive to change his paradigm!)

Your incentive to change is a whole new second adulthood. A clean slate. A chance to break out of the traditional boundaries of age, identity, and time. Go back over these three areas and determine what your present paradigm is. Do you think of yourself as old? When you look into the future is it downhill? Is your identity trimmed in chrome and capable of hitting sixty miles per hour in five seconds? Are you still trying to cram twenty-five hours into twenty-four? If so, you will need to make some changes in the way you view these things if you want the second half of your life to be immeasurably better than the first.

Part 3

Back in the Game

We are on the brink of discovery. In Willa Cather's O Pioneers!, *it was the open land of the American West that gave drive and purpose to so many lives. At the dawn of a new century, it is the adult life cycle itself—stretching it, taming it, bringing it under control, making it yield its riches—that beckons us all, men and women alike. This is the new human frontier.*

Gail Sheehy, *New Passages*

The two most common mistakes made by people who want to shift from success to significance are to stay in the first half or to never leave halftime. You have chosen to enter the locker room at the end of your first half and have assessed your situation in the biggest game of your life. The time you have spent choosing what's in the box, creating a mission statement, forming a team, and putting together a game plan have positioned you to do things beyond your wildest imagination.

To sell its brand of athletic shoes and equipment, Nike has tapped into a sentiment that is so appropriate for you at this stage in your life: just do it. There comes a time when you have to say to yourself, "I may not have all the answers yet, and I'm not exactly sure where this is going to go, but that's okay. I'm going to take charge of the second half of my life and go for it!"

Straight ahead lie the greatest years of your life.

14

It Really Doesn't Get Any Better Than This

When the Israelites finally came within striking distance of the Promised Land, they sent ten men to go behind the lines to see what it was like. Eight returned with a frightening picture of what lay ahead. Two delivered a completely different picture. They all saw the same things but disagreed on whether what they saw was good or bad.

You are on the border of the Promised Land, and I have been your spy to tell you about what's on the other side of the river. I have told you about the rich fruit, the milk and honey, the wide and glorious rivers. I have told you about the giants but have assured you they can be slain.

Perhaps you have heard other voices telling you what to expect in your fifties, sixties, seventies, and beyond, and like the Israelites you are wavering. I would like to conclude this book with a few notes of courage, because I know how easy it is to remain in the wilderness.

WHY IT'S BETTER

I realize that in our culture of youth it is somewhat revolutionary to suggest that the second half of your life can be better than the first. But it really can. I can think of at least seven reasons why:

First, *you are less likely to be diverted by things that don't matter.* In chapter 8 I referred to a series of concentric circles that represent ways in which our needs are met. The outer circle represents the making and spending of money. The next circle represents accomplishments. In the next circle are the needs that can only be satisfied by relationships with your spouse, children, and those who are very close to you. The inner circle represents those needs that can be met only by the transcendent. They're what Jesus referred to when he used metaphors like the "bread of life" and "living water." In the second half you know more about the importance of the inner two circles. You have a greater sense of balance in your life, knowing what's central and what's marginal, and how much time to spend in each circle.

Second, *you are finally able to live out your own agenda rather than someone else's.* In the first half, we think our agenda is to get a job and put the skills we learned in college to use. That's a deceptive sense of self-realization. It is living by someone else's agenda, which is inevitable because you do need to make a living. Plus, you may not even know what your agenda is. One of the things you may be hearing in that still, small voice is, "I knit you together with very special material and it's not being used the way I intended."

Third, *you will regain control of your life.* Imagine what it will be like to be able to say no. In the past that has been difficult because you had not thought through your "one thing." It all looked pretty good to you and probably *was* good. But now that you have identified your mainspring, you can choose to give yourself in a focused way to that which supports your mission. That is immeasurably liberating.

Fourth, *you have more resources.* Most people in their fourth or fifth decades have built up some reserve to provide security. You have a much larger knowledge base, a network. You know how to work smarter versus working harder, and all these resources make this time of your life better, even if you don't pursue a halftime mission.

Fifth, *you can have a clean slate—an opportunity for a new beginning.* Do you really want to go back to the way you've been living in the first half? You're one of the first generations in America to have a second adulthood ahead of them. You really can expect to have at least twenty more years of good health, an active mind, and opportunities for growth. Have you ever said, "If only I knew then what I know now?" In a sense, you do. Think about it.

Sixth, *you know how to play through pain.* Things that might have laid you low in the first half will not be as devastating to you. You're tougher, mentally and spiritually. There's a statistic kept in the National Football League known as YAC—yards after contact. It records the number of yards a running back covers after he's been hit. I believe one thing we know in our fifties that we didn't know in our twenties is that we can take a hit and keep going. That's a tremendous comfort as you head out into the unknown.

And seventh, *you have finally learned about grace.* The first half teaches that you have to do it on your own, where the second half shows you that you're covered if you fail. I like to explain grace to people this way: On a scale of one to one hundred, with one hundred being perfect, where would you place yourself? Where would you place an axe-murderer? A saint? Mother Teresa might rank as high as ninety or ninety-five, and the ax-murderer would probably drop somewhere near ten. (He's bound to have helped his grandmother across the street one day.) You rank somewhere in between. But each of you gets the same gift: grace. As the New Testament explains it, grace makes up the difference so that you score a perfect one hundred.

STAY ALERT

As you proceed in your second-half journey, there are a few obstacles of which you should be aware:

Job Creep

You are so good at what you have done in the first half that it constantly beckons you back and is comfortable and familiar. But just because you can do something well doesn't mean you must stick with it in the same manner the rest of your life.

I confess there are times I envy those guys who are still running up the score, reaping fortunes, and appearing on magazine covers as superstar executives running growing companies. When those feelings set in, you need to say, "first things first and last things not at all." You need to focus on what is really important in *this* season of your life. Otherwise, you will be right back in the first-half mode . . . only a little older.

Isolation

If you significantly alter your employment picture, you may miss the camaraderie that comes with working out of an office with colleagues and support staff. Don't underestimate this potential loss, because the importance of relationships becomes more evident as you head into the second half. The best way to combat this obstacle is to make sure you have built a team to journey with you and that you consult with them regularly.

Absence or Change of Routine

Humans are creatures of habit, often more than we like to admit. If you've gotten up at 6:30 A.M. every day for the past twenty years, showered, stopped for coffee, and taken the elevator to your office, you may not handle a less structured schedule very well. Some people find they need a routine in order to be productive. When they change their relationship with their employer and reduce their other commitments, their "free time" initially results in some time management problems. They find they do not use that time very wisely. You may need to keep your regular schedule, even if you no longer are required to go into your office every day at eight.

Availability

I've warned you earlier, but it bears repeating. As soon as people hear that you've altered your life in order to pursue your own agenda, they will assume that means you want to help them either by making a significant donation or by joining their board, or both. This can be a blessing and a curse. You may indeed want to find organizations with whom you can partner to reach mutually-held goals, but you don't want to go on overload, either. I've found that it helps to operate your second-half mission as if it were a business. Take only those appointments that fit your new second-half focus. Evaluate the proposals that are presented to you and make decisions based on your core principles and beliefs.

IT REALLY DOESN'T GET ANY BETTER THAN THIS

Even with the potential roadblocks, I have to confess that this is my favorite time of life. In my first half, I took a lot of satisfaction in running up the score. I loved making my business grow, seeing the bottom line increase, and adding to the value of my company. The blessedness of the second half is that I still get to run up the score. And I'm still seeing my business grow, but I'm investing in something bigger than cable television.

The work really is the thing that makes the second half vivid and exciting. I'm not rationalizing when I say that this really is the best time of our lives if we will see it so and act on our beliefs. The second half is a great epic journey of a mature life, and the work itself is its own dividend. Sure it's a risk. But with the risk comes adventure. So I close this book with the hope that you will take time to let God give you a vision of what the Promised Land means to you personally. That you will pull the trigger. Jump off the high dive. Leave the comfort and security of home. Cross the wilderness!

And that at the end of the hero's journey on this earth and the beginning of your life in eternity you can say to yourself, "The time of my departure is at hand . . . I have fought the good fight . . . I have finished the race . . . I have kept the faith."

And that in response you will hear a grand voice say:

"Well done, good and faithful servant. You have been faithful over a few things. Now I will make you ruler over many things. Come and receive the crown of righteousness which I have laid up for you this day."

Frequently Asked Questions

Whenever I speak about the halftime experience, people come up to me afterward with questions. I suspect you, too, may have some questions, and in the next few pages I will try to anticipate and answer them for you.

Do I need to quit my job in order to have the kind of second half you describe?

You don't have to quit your job, but you may need to renegotiate how you work. If your job requires your attention for forty or more hours a week, trying to do what is recommended in this book will only cause more frustration than you are already feeling. In most cases, successful second halfers who are still with their first-half employer have negotiated their commitment to half- or three-quarter time. An increasingly popular option is the home office, which often allows workers to complete their work in less time because they have fewer interruptions and are exempt from many meetings. Different physical locations are right for different types of work. For example, the office is most often the best place for "buffer days," a client's office the best place for "focus days," and a second home or cottage the best place for "free days."

Having said all that, if your work is a constant source of frustration, you will need to deal with that before you enter the second half. That *could* mean leaving your present work, but it may also mean a horizontal move within your company into an area that suits you better. Think about what results and performance you really contribute to your work and focus exclusively on that.

But I really love my job. Can't I stay with it into the second half?

If you like your job and can use it as a vehicle to support what's in the box, yes. The best example of how this can happen is Bruce Brookshire, chairman of a chain of grocery stores based in Tyler, Texas. When you walk into a Brookshire grocery store, you will immediately notice a difference in the employees. They are courteous and responsive, they appear to like their jobs, they interact with customers, and they seem to have real pride in their work. This is no small feat in the retail world. It happens because it has been Bruce's mission. Here's a case where he has been able to make the transition from success to significance without leaving a job he loved and the people he loved being with and serving. Another wonderful example is Bill Pollard, chairman of ServiceMaster, a company that has grown fifty percent annually based on four principles: (1) to honor God in all we do; (2) to help people develop; (3) to pursue excellence; and (4) to grow profitably. ServiceMaster is Bill Pollard's significance career.

Do you have to be a millionaire to have a successful second half?

The parable of the talents (Matt. 25:14–30) teaches that each of the three servants was given an assignment "each according to his own ability," and that the servant who multiplied two talents was honored just as much as the servant who multiplied five talents. It was only the servant who buried his talent in the ground who was firmly rebuked.

When we come to the end of our time here on earth and the beginning of our journey in eternity, the Bible teaches us that we will each—individually, one at a time—stand before God to give a final accounting for our lives. I visualize the final exam consisting of two questions: (1) Did you believe (or did you turn your back and walk away)? and (2) What did you do with what I gave *you* to work with (not the church, not your family, not the government, not the fortune I gave someone else to work with, but what did you do with the time, talent, and treasure I gave *you* to work with)?

This book is a preparation for that examination.

I'm in my late fifties. Is it too late to enter halftime?

Not at all. I know people who are in their sixties who have decided to change and realize they could have twenty years of second-half significance. The question is not is it too late, but do you really want to keep doing what you are doing? I suspect that many people in their sixties will almost fall into halftime by default once they realize retirement is either impossible, undesirable, or downright dangerous to their helath and longevity. In other words, instead of going to work at MacDonald's, we'll see more "seniors" retool for another ten to twenty years of significance.

Is halftime and a significant second half only for men?

No, but I don't fully understand the timetable under which women may be operating. For the woman who enters the professional world out of college and stays there, I have a hunch that pretty much everything about halftime and the second half applies to them. An interesting phenomenon I have observed is the woman who is an "empty nester." Having raised her children, she is now ready to enter a new career. Some of these women may be reversing the male pattern by having significance in the first half and success in the second. Personally, I don't think halftime is a gender issue as much as a "life circumstance" issue.

I was just beginning to look forward to retirement. What's wrong with taking it easy after putting in so many years of hard work?

We have to be careful with the idea that the object of work is to earn enough money so we can lead a life of leisure. Work itself can be a reward. As Fred Smith Sr. once told me, "Work is the psychological glue that holds a man together." Retirement is simply not good for one's mental health. There's a fascinating study in the book *Flow,* by Mihaly Csikzentmihalyi. The author attached beepers to individuals and polled their levels of satisfaction at different times. Although they all expressed a desire for more leisure time, they actually expressed much higher levels of satisfaction while they were working in the pursuit of some meaningful goal than when they were engaged in sedentary activity. Interesting!

The zone that the author calls "flow" is in between the zone of anxiety on one side and the zone of boredom on the other.

The author says that "every flow activity, whether it involved competition, chance, or any other dimension of experience, had this in common: It provided a sense of discovery, a creative feeling of transporting the person into a new reality. It pushed the person to higher levels of performance and led to previously unheard of states of consciousness. In short, it transformed the self by making it more complex. In this growth of the self lies the key to flow activities."

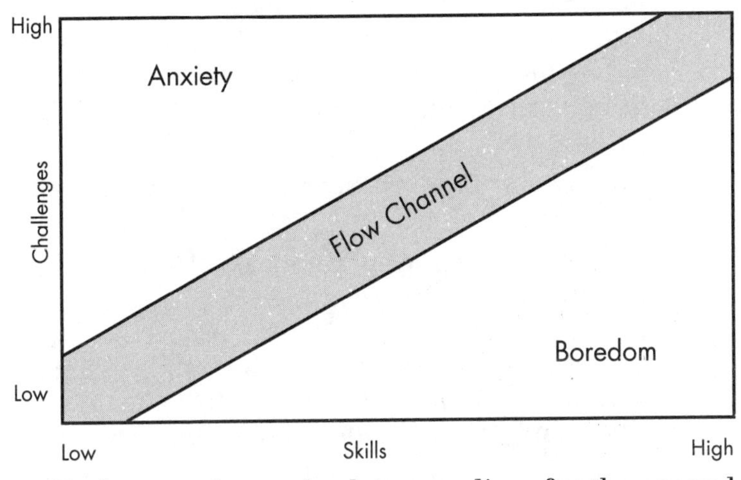

Retirement is an obsolete paradigm for the second half. We *need* work.

Is halftime always preceded by a crisis?

Not always. In my case, I think I would have still entered halftime had I not lost my son. His death may have accelerated a process that had already begun. This tragedy, along with two other "interventions," just gave this process a sense of urgency for me. By the time most people are fifty, they have taken a pretty big hit below the water line—a divorce, a death, betrayal by a trusted friend or colleague, the loss of a job, a health event. These things do tend to make you think about what really matters in your life. But even without these things, I think it is natural for those in their fourth decade to begin examining their lives more deeply.

Dr. James Dobson refers to midlife as a time of reevaluation and new opportunity rather than a time of crisis. "Midlife crisis" was a trendy phrase that caught on with the media, but it doesn't accurately describe my halftime or that which I observe in many, many others. You don't need to wait for something bad to happen in order to enter halftime. You can self-initiate your own wake-up call.

Once I launch out into my second-half adventure, can I change directions?

Absolutely. Don't think of your second half as another job with a gold watch waiting for you at the end. I know men who are on their third project in a second half that is only five years old. The beauty of the second half is that you really do call the shots. It's your agenda, and you can change it whenever you see fit.

One word of caution. While your projects may change, your mission shouldn't—at least not drastically. If your mission is constantly changing, you did not do your homework on your game plan and may need to return to halftime. But that's okay too. Go back to the box, determine your one thing, and create a new mission statement. Allow yourself to discover what's right for you by trial and error.

Is it possible to be in the first half and the second at the same time?

Yes, but not for long. In fact, many people have one foot on either side. I consider it a form of seismic testing or parallel career. Sometimes it reflects an understandable ambivalence about leaving the excitement of the first half (Do I really want to give up the corner office?). Eventually, however, you will come to a point where the first half will seem increasingly adolescent and out of season. Then it's time to move on to the next adventure, forcefully, not reluctantly!

Your passion seems so other directed. You really seem to want to help others. I don't feel that way. When I consider a second half, I want to do something for me. Am I just selfish?

Doing something for you and doing something for others are not opposite ends of a continuum. The whole point of altruistic egotism is that when you help others you help yourself even more.

Remember, too, that the starting point in halftime is you. What do *you* want to do with the rest of your life? That's the great benefit of the second half. You're doing what you are created to do and what you're good at doing. I simply believe that ultimately you will be happier if you can find a way to connect what you like to do with what needs to be done—or as I prefer to say it, with God's larger story.

I can understand your resistance if you begin with the question, "What can I do to help others?" But if you begin with, "What do I want to do?" I think you will eventually see the value in directing that activity into something bigger than just you.

How can I be sure that the mission I have chosen will work?

You can't, really. The significance quest in the second half is about risk and adventure . . . and faith. At some point you just have to launch out and see what happens. But there are ways to minimize risk: seismic testing, listening to your team and the input of others, trying a pilot project before rolling it out on a larger scale. As they say, crawl, walk, run.

Peter Drucker has given me three invaluable pieces of advice about starting something new. First, build on islands of health and strength, meaning don't try to make something happen in an area that has been plagued by failure. Instead, help bring something into being that is trying to happen anyway. Second, deal only with people who are receptive to what you're trying to do. And third, focus only on those things that will make a big difference if you are successful. These three pieces of advice have become the core principles that guide everything I do in my second half.

You seem to put a lot of emphasis on solitude, free time, reflection. I'm not wired that way. Does that mean I won't benefit from halftime?

Everyone will have some type of midlife experience. Whether or not you benefit from it is determined by whether you control it (halftime) or it controls you (crisis). Certainly personality and temperament will play a role in how you structure your game plan. But don't be too quick to say you weren't wired for reflection. I didn't think I was able to spend so much free time when I was in my first half, but I have learned the value of quiet contemplation.

You may not need as much reflective time as I do, but if you deny yourself this resource I doubt that you will make a safe transition to significance. I tend to agree with Pascal, who said, "All the world's ills stem from the fact that a man cannot sit in a room alone."

I know you aren't a theologian, but do you worry that you might be emphasizing works over belief?

Not at all. Most Christians—especially those who are called evangelical—know what they believe. Americans have been given a tremendous opportunity to understand what they believe. They have heard sermons, read books, and listened to tapes that explain their faith. What we haven't had are opportunities to act out those beliefs in ways that connect to our true selves. People of faith aren't asking about what they believe; they're asking what they can do with what they believe. And most of the work Christians are asked to do is relatively insignificant. I mean, if you have an advertising executive in your congregation don't just ask him to come rake leaves on a Saturday morning. I don't think we have to worry about people of faith doing too much good.

I really resonate with your advice to clear my plate. But I serve on my church board, my school board, I teach a Sunday school class and coach a Little League team. How do I leave those important things without disappointing people?

You can't. People will naturally be disappointed if they lose a valuable contributor to their mission. But one of the humbling truths I have learned in this regard is that I'm really not indispensable. After I leave a board, there's someone who will come along who will do a better job than I did. What's more, if you stay too busy with other peoples' agendas, who will care for yours? Ultimately, you will do more good if you have more time to focus on your own agenda.

Epilogue

Those who read *Halftime* and *Game Plan* often want to know more about the endeavors in which I am involved as a result of my own halftime experience. What follows is a brief description of four initiatives that reflect my interests both as an entrepreneur and as someone wanting to make a difference through the application of my faith and resources under the general mission of transforming the latent energy of the American church into active energy. For more information on a specific initiative, I have included their telephone numbers and addresses and would encourage you to directly contact the appropriate organization.

LEADERSHIP NETWORK

Leadership Network is a private operating foundation I created in 1984 for the original purpose of identifying, networking, and resourcing senior ministers and staff of large congregations (1,000+ in attendance) in the United States. The churches represent a wide variety of Protestant faith traditions that range from mainline to evangelical to independent and are characterized by their innovation, desire to be on the cutting edge of ministry, and entrepreneurial leadership.

The mission of Leadership Network is to be the resource broker that supplies information to and connects leaders of innovative churches. We believe the emerging new paradigm of the twenty-first century church calls for the development of new tools and resources as well as the equipping of a new type of twenty-first century leader, both clergy and laity. This new reformation is not centered in theology but rather is focused on structure, organization, and the transition from an institutional-based church to a mission-driven church. Undergirding all of our activities is a desire to foster excellence in applied ministry that results in transformed lives.

In recent years, we have expanded our original constituency to include major initiatives in lay mobilization, in denominational leadership at the middle and regional judicatory level, and in identifying and resourcing the next generation of emerging young leaders.

To contact Leadership Network, call 1-800-765-5323 or e-mail them at http:\\www.leadnet.org.

LEADERSHIP TRAINING NETWORK

Believing that one of the hallmarks of a twenty-first century church is its engagement and deployment of the laity in ministry and mission, the Leadership Training Network (LTN) was created in 1995. It has as its purpose to identify, train, and provide an ongoing peer coaching network for leaders of lay mobilization in local congregations. Through its training programs, materials, and consultations, LTN is making a distinct contribuiton to the emerging twenty-first century church.

For more information on the Leadership Training Network, call 1-800-765-5323 or e-mail to http:\\www.leadnet.org.

THE PETER F. DRUCKER FOUNDATION FOR NONPROFIT MANAGEMENT

In 1988, Dick Shubert, Frances Hesselbein, and I convinced Peter Drucker to lend his name, his great mind, and occasionally his presence to establish an operating foundation for the purpose of leading social sector organizations toward excellence in performance. I serve as Founding Chairman of the Board of Governors.

The Drucker Foundation believes that a healthy society requires three sectors: a public sector of effective governments; a private sector of effective businesses; and a social sector of effective community organizations. While the three sectors are, and must be, autonomous, they are also interdependent. The Drucker Foundation also believes that in American society at the present time, it is the social sector which has not only the greatest potential for healthy growth and opportunities for contribution, but also faces the greatest challenges. Through its conferences, publications, and partnerships, the Drucker Foundation is helping social sector organizations focus on their mission, achieve true accountability, leverage innovation, and develop productive partnerships.

For more information, write or call The Drucker Foundation, 320 Park Avenue, 3rd floor, New York, NY 10022-6839. Telephone (212) 224-1174 or E-mail at druckerf@ix.netcom.com.

SOCIAL ENTREPRENEUR'S INITIATIVE

I have personally followed at one time or another each of the eight pathways I set out earlier in *Game Plan.* In this season of my life, I am concentrating on being a social entrepreneur by forming initiatives which I hope will be of service and address needs in society and communities across the nation. In keeping with my own "wiring," my role is more of an entrepreneur for the ideas rather than a donor, and I have begun to form a network of social entrepreneurs. By definition, a social entrepreneur is an individual in halftime or the second half with sufficient capacity, who wants to use their resources to conceive and grow innovative ventures that meet social needs.

I believe our nation is populated with thousands of such people. If this is what you are doing or would like to do, and you would like to be networked with others of like intentions, please contact me at Leadership Network, 1-800-765-5323 or E-mail me at http:\\www.leadnet.org.

Acknowledgments

For this book and *Halftime*, I have most of all to thank the people at Zondervan Publishing House: Scott Bolinder, for persuading me to spend the time and hard labor; Lyn Cryderman, for his wonderful way with words; and John Sloan and Rachel Boers, for wise editing. My assistant, BJ Engle, did good work in rendering legible my scratchings on pages and pages of legal pads and hotel stationery. Many contributions of useful questions, models, and exercises are also acknowledged throughout this book.

Once again I discovered that not only this book but everything I have done that counts for anything has been done in the context of a team. God just didn't build us to function alone. I owe so much to so many. In *Halftime* I acknowledged over one hundred people by name. All of them, save one ("into each life a little rain must fall"), are still there for me, playing important roles in my life. I invite you to pick up your copy of *Halftime* to once again celebrate with me the joy of being surrounded by such a cloud of good people—wise counselors, comrades-in-arms, valued associates.

Most of the "new" people I want to acknowledge are those like Terry Warren, whose letter begins chapter 1 of this book, for taking the time to write or say a word of thanks for *Halftime*. It feels like I have learned more about halftime since the book was released (now over 70,000 copies in print) than before. I have been the recipient of so many halftime stories. It has been largely in response to the comment, "Okay. I'm in halftime. Now give me the specifics of how I can find the pathway to significance in my second half" that I undertook the book you now hold in your hands.

The most important people in my life are my wife, Linda, still the most attractive woman in the world to me, and Peter Drucker, my coach and wise guide. Peter should win the Nobel Peace Prize. His ideas, more than anyone else's, have had much to do with preserving the fifty years of world peace in which I have been privileged to live. Management is the X-factor in each segment of our free and democratic society, and Peter Drucker is the father of modern management. He's also the best example I know of someone with a significant second half.

But most of all I want to thank God. I quoted George Bernard Shaw in *Halftime*, saying, "This is the true joy in life—being used for a purpose recognized by yourself as a mighty one," and that's just what has happened to me. I know I had something to do with *Halftime*, but is seems, in retrospect, as if it were mainly making myself available. I always felt more like the cloth in a sail being filled and carried forth by a wind that provided the real power. True, the sail is important, but the wind much more so. What a ride this second half is! And I am not kidding myself about where the credit belongs.

Good job, God!

We hope you've enjoyed *Game Plan.* If you have, we are confident that you'll also enjoy Bob Buford's first book, *Halftime,* the book that has helped create a movement!

HALFTIME Softcover.
ISBN 0-310-21532-3

Since it was first introduced, this book has occupied a unique place on the desks of thousands of business executives and managers. These men and women already have experienced much success and are now seeking meaning and significance in their lives and relationships.

This groundbreaking book is now available in quality paperback at an affordable price for group use and as a life-changing gift.

Also available:

HALFTIME / GAME PLAN
audio pages 2 90-minute audio cassettes.
ISBN 0-310-21583-8

As an extension of *Halftime, Game Plan* is a personal and practical guide for men and women who want to apply the principles of *Halftime* in their daily lives. Here for the first time is an audio tape package containing two 90-minute cassettes combining the content of both *Halftime* and *Game Plan* into the highly portable audio format perfect for listening while traveling, commuting, or exercising.

ZondervanPublishingHouse
Grand Rapids, Michigan
http://www.zondervan.com
A Division of HarperCollins*Publishers*

We want to hear from you. Please send your comments about this book to us in care of the address below. Thank you.

ZondervanPublishingHouse
Grand Rapids, Michigan 49530
http://www.zondervan.com